# THE
# MIRACLE
# SEASON

Caroline "Line" Found
June 19, 1994 - August 11, 2011

# THE MIRACLE SEASON

KATHY BRESNAHAN

**KCI** *SPORTS PUBLISHING*

ISBN:  1-940056-48-7
ISBN 13:  978-1-940056-48-7

This book is available in quantity at special discounts for your group or organization. For further information, contact:

**KCI** *SPORTS PUBLISHING*

3340 Whiting Avenue, Suite 5
Stevens Point, WI  54481
www.kcisports.com

*Photos courtesy of:* Mike Jenn, Adam Canady, Kathy Bresnahan, Cedar Rapids Gazette, USA Today/Gannett, Matthew Holst, Ernie Found, Olivia Mekies and Kelly Fliehler

*Bonus Movie Section photos:* photos by Cate Cameron, courtesy of LD Entertainment. Kathy behind the camera, by Pat Smith.

*Cover Design:* Nicky Brillowski
*Book Layout and Design:* Nicky Brillowski

Printed and bound in the United States.

# DEDICATION

To the coaches in my life: Sue Wehnke, Cathy Williams, Nancy Ostergaard, JJ Horvath, Jennifer Berna, Gene Vaassen, Nubs Vaassen, Fred Pedersen, Shelley George, Jim Neis and my most important coaches – Dan and Darlene Bresnahan: thanks for your patience, guidance, and influence. You were tremendous role models.

To all my volleyball, basketball, softball and tennis teammates: thanks for the championships but more importantly, the enduring support and friendship.

To all my former athletes from Benton, WI and Iowa City West: thanks for your passion, commitment, and all the great memories. You each have a place in my heart.

To Line: thanks for making me a better person.

# ACKNOWLEDGEMENTS

It's been four years since I first started writing about our remarkable 2011 volleyball season and my admiration for professional writers has increased tenfold – what a grueling process. So many tears were shed as I relived practices, games and the emotional breakdowns – and I quickly learned that recounting the events was the easy part of this process. Ignorance is bliss... I had no idea how difficult it would be to make this story speak to others. The final manuscript (fortunately) doesn't resemble the initial attempts to write a book and that is because of the help of so many others.

Many thanks to my great friends Pat Smith and Jan Leff who read and reread my first feeble attempts and offered valuable insight.

Mary Allen, "Ye Olde Writing Coach", you patiently pulled me in the right direction while admonishing me to 'describe the moment' for the reader. This book wouldn't have been completed without your expertise and guidance.

I have a hard time imagining that there's a better editor than Betsy Thorpe. Her humor, empathy and objectivity gave me hope.

Thank you Peter Clark and KCI Publishing for seeing the potential in this book. Your unwavering support and professionalism made this dream a reality.

Finally, to my guys from LD Entertainment: Mickey Liddell, Scott Holyrod and Pete Shilaimon – thanks for sticking with us and telling this story to the world. I'll love you forever.

# TABLE OF CONTENTS

# FOREWORD

For everyone who knew and loved Caroline Found, what promised to be a long, wild and slightly zany ride got cut impossibly short on August 11th, 2011. Caroline's death seemed to qualify as a violation of the laws of physics. How could this bright, golden-haired, peripatetic force of nature – how could she, of all people, be stilled?

The irony rests in death's ability to stop the unstoppable, to dominate the indomitable. Ask anyone who met Line (and I have asked quite a few) and they will tell you that her energy and enthusiasm could power an entire town, let alone a high school volleyball team. Her passing, as a result, left many people in the dark.

As coach of Caroline's beloved West High Trojans, Kathy Bresnahan was tasked with turning the lights back on. For one remarkable season, Brez led Line's teammates in a battle, not against a few dozen other opponents, but against the spectre of Caroline's disappearance from their teenaged world. When waves of grief knocked the team down, Brez, in their midst, helped them to stand up. She wept with them. She consoled them. And she coached them, these fifteen volleyball players, without once thinking they could somehow repeat as state champions. Brez focused instead on the task at hand: mending her team's shattered connection to life and to living by playing a game with a ball and a net. Ask her how she did it and she'd probably tell you there was no plan, no map, just a Midwestern gal making it up as she went along.

Having gotten to know Brez over the last few years, I can weigh in on what transpired. Good coaches combine the skillsets of teachers, therapists, disciplinarians and cheerleaders. They know how to listen. How to speak the truth when needed. How and when to bring out the best in everyone. Brez is that kind of coach. But what made her journey so unique (and challenging) was having to throw out a lifetime of coaching experience in the aftermath of Caroline's death. You can't demand more reps, more hours of practice, more discipline from the fragile psyches of grieving athletes. You have to find another way.

Brez's story, powerfully told in the pages that follow, is all about finding that way. Our own paths crossed when a film production company optioned the rights to Caroline's story and hired me to write the screenplay. After meeting first with Line's irrepressible dad, Ernie Found, I flew out to Iowa City in March of 2014. Brez immediately opened her heart to me and to everyone who came after. And as I returned to Iowa that year and the next, I got to cherish our growing friendship.

The more time I spent with Brez and with her memories of Caroline, the more it struck me by how much the two of them shared in common: extroverts who craved an audience while secretly being shy and private people; athletes and leaders who challenged everyone around them to rise to the next level; and, lastly and most tellingly, comedians with a similarly wacky and irresistible sense of humor – the kind that even while poking fun at others, never left anyone feeling excluded. Being around Brez, I soon discovered, meant laughing a lot. Turns out that in a story with so much death and loss, it really helps to be funny.

Movies often have as their subjects ordinary people doing extraordinary things. This story is no exception. What stands out is the sheer number of people who, in addition to Kathy Bresnahan, rose to other worldly heights: Ernie and Ellyn Found, Kelley Fliehler, Line's core teammates and their parents, West High administrators and the student body, not to mention volleyball players and coaches from across the Hawkeye state. Caroline's comet dimmed, but her community rose up together to shine a luminous light on everyone who knew her, and many more (like myself) who never had that pleasure.

Brez's story about the 2011 season inspires all of us with the message that Caroline modeled every day of her 17 years. We are all called to Live Like Line.

**David Aaron Cohen**
Screenwriter, *Friday Night Lights*
December, 2016
Los Angeles, California

# A LETTER FROM CAROLINE

*It hit me when I was halfway through my sophomore year at West, here at the big, stressful, chaotic building of bricks. As I walked into advisory one Thursday morning, my eyes were searching for the delicious brownies or candy Mrs. Kanellis brought to us every Thursday, but instead I was handed a college guide packet.*

*A college packet?!?! What!?!? I am a sophomore; I am still a little kid!!! I still have people cut my meat for me; I still believe in Santa Claus, I love Toys R Us, WHAT!?!? I don't even think about college.*

*I never thought this time would come, I try to avoid it every day, but avoiding can only work for so long. I know it's here, the time has come. I am a big kid now; the "I'm trying to make you more independent for college" remark comes out of my mother's mouth more than monthly now. It's more of a daily thing. Yes mother, I know. But I will always have you there to hold my hand when I take a big step or make a hard decision right? I'll still give you my Christmas list every year to send to Santa? As much as I hope for this answer to be yes, I know that I am taking my first steps into the "individuality" thing and entering the world of college and my own life. But, as we all stack up on as many honors and AP classes, volunteer hours and college credit opportunities as we can, remember one thing: don't let the facts get in the way of your imagination.*

*I am often thought of as childish. I prefer to interpret that as child-like. I still get wildly enthusiastic about little* things. I tend to exaggerate and fantasize and think big. I still watch cartoons when I can. I play with leaves. I skip down the street and sing to myself. I can't go outside without getting dirty. I believe in Santa Claus. And that is something I will never, EVER let go of. Often I am told, that "IF Santa were real, he would have to travel to 91 million households in 24 hours blah blah blah blah." SO WHAT!?! I mean, it's the fun and imagination that counts. Just because we don't understand something and it's not actually possible, doesn't mean it ain't so! Wikipedia believes in Santa. If they didn't, why would they have a whole page dedicated to Santa Claus?

When I was little I had this idea that life could be perfect. That if you were careful enough, you'd never make a mistake, never be lonely, never be misunderstood, never be frightened, but it doesn't work that way. Life is big and messy, and you just have to climb in it with your boots on and hope for the best. But we all know that things won't always turn out perfectly, and we can't always take life the easy way. No more bed-time stories and naps after lunch time.

So it is time to grow up, literally, meaning taking the college courses, doing interviews for jobs, and being a role model for others. But that doesn't mean we have to let go of the things we once thought of as a little kid with a big imagination.

Children have neither past nor future, they enjoy the present, which very few of us do. So stop and smell the roses, sing to yourself, and enjoy what we have, while we have it.

**Caroline Found**
*West Side Story Sports editor*
*December. 17, 2010*
*Volume 42, Issue 3*

*Reprinted by permission of West Side Story*

# PROLOGUE
## AUGUST 12, 2011

The shrill ring of the phone startles me from a deep sleep. I look at the clock: it's 12:43 a.m. Who could possibly be calling? Something must be wrong. I push my dog Charlie's head off my arm and grab the phone off the nightstand.

"Hello?" I whisper into the phone, my heart racing.

"Brez, this is Shelly." I'm immediately angry: Line and Shelly have woken me up again.

Caroline Found and Shelly Stumpff are senior starters on the volleyball team I coach at Iowa City West High School. Both big jokesters, they love having fun at my expense. I didn't mind when they called in the middle of the night a couple of times over the summer; it was kind of funny. But I'm exhausted from wrapping up our first week of pre-season volleyball. My blood pressure is rising and I decide to hang up on the two of them before they can say anything.

"Wait, don't hang up," Shelly says. "Kelley's with me. There's been an accident." She pauses. I hear her voice breaking up, "Caroline was riding a moped and crashed into a tree. She died."

I know this is another typical Caroline joke, albeit a sick one. "Come on, you guys, this isn't funny. You two will pay for this in the morning. I'm going back to sleep now."

"Seriously, don't hang up, it really happened!" Shelly yells. Then all I can hear is Kelley's heart-wrenching screams in the background. I can't take in what Shelly just said. Caroline's dead? My mind refuses to wrap itself around the words. There must be some mistake.

"Shelly, let me talk to your mom," I say.

I hear Shelly tell her mother that I want to talk to her.

"Hi Brez, this is Kathy. It's true. Caroline apparently borrowed a moped from a friend and was coming home from a Young Life meeting. She lost control and hit a tree. Nobody knows exactly what happened, but it's true – she died. The girls and their parents are starting to gather here."

I reach over Charlie and try to find the switch for the lamp. Charlie gently thumps his tail on the bed. I fumble around for the lamp and somehow knock it on the floor. One part of my brain registers that the bulb shattered, but I don't even look down at it as I crawl over Charlie and get out of bed. I flip on the overhead light – my eyes reflexively close in protest. None of this can be true. Surely there must be a mistake and the girls meant to say that Ellyn has died. Ellyn, Caroline's mother, was diagnosed with stage-four pancreatic cancer four months ago and her health has been rapidly deteriorating.

"Kathy, please let me talk to the girls again," I say into the phone.

The sobs in the background subside. "Hello?" Kelley Fliehler says quietly. I can hear her breathing, trying to catch her breath.

"Kelley, where are you right now? Should we call everyone and get together as a team?"

"No, let's wait until the morning. We're all here at my house. Our parents are with us."

"Okay, I understand. Please call if you want me to come over, otherwise I'll see all of you tomorrow at 7:30."

The phone feels contaminated. I throw it down on the bed. I grab some warmer clothes and put them on. I have no idea what I should do. Call my assistant coach,

Scott Sanders, who's worked with our program the past two years? Go over to the Fliehler's house? Get ahold of one of my friends? It's impossible to wrap my mind around this news. Then I feel incredible anger, I can't breathe. The room is closing in on me.

I carefully sidestep the broken shards of light bulb on the floor. "Come on, Charlie," I say, and he and I walk outside to the gazebo. The cool night air helps to clear my head. I decide to call Scott and tell him this unfathomable news.

I can barely punch in his phone number, my hands are shaking so badly. The phone rings for a long time and then he answers, his voice thick with sleep.

"Scott, brace yourself. I have the most horrible news possible. Caroline was in an accident tonight and died."

His reaction is identical to mine: disbelief. We talk for a while and his voice changes as the news sinks in and he's hit with his own wave of overwhelming grief. I can tell he's on the verge of crying, but know he won't cry until he hangs up. He asks me if he should text the other team members with the news, in case some of them haven't heard yet; we agree we don't want anyone who still hadn't heard showing up for practice tomorrow. We were especially concerned about some of the younger players who may not be part of the seniors' circle of communication. I tell him I'll text everyone. We agree to meet at six a.m. in my office at West High School. I hang up the phone and bury my head in Charlie's soft red coat. Then I set about the impossible task of figuring out how to tell these young women that we've lost the heart and soul of our team, the girl who always makes us laugh and brightens all our days.

Finally, I finish writing the text and push send. I lean back against the rattan bench, rest my head against Charlie's side, and begin to cry.

## CHAPTER 1

# CAROLINE

Two coaches changed my life.

In high school, Sue Wehnke, our track coach, and Cathy Williams, our basketball coach, taught me that it was all right to be a female athlete, even though back then, in the mid-1970s, athletic opportunities for women were still just beginning to emerge. They inspired and influenced the course of my life: I decided I wanted to be a teacher and a coach.

I played volleyball and basketball my four years at the University of Wisconsin-Platteville, and loved the shared experiences, the laughs. I wanted to keep having those kinds of experiences for the rest of my life, and offer similar opportunities to future female athletes.

I was hired to teach Health and Physical Education and coach varsity volleyball at West High in Iowa City. Iowa City is located in east central Iowa, and nestles up next to the scenic Iowa River. The fifth-largest town in Iowa with 75,000 residents and the county seat, it was once recognized by *Forbes* magazine as the second-best small metropolitan area for doing business in the United States. Here we enjoy tree-lined streets, a quaint downtown business area and enough parks, bike trails and boating in the nearby Coralville Lake Reservoir to satisfy the most ardent outdoor enthusiast.

The main attraction in town is the University of Iowa, which includes the University of Iowa Hospital and Clinics, and spans 1700 acres on each side of the river.

Each fall the town's population increases 50% as over 30,000 graduate and undergraduate students flood the area. Much of the excitement in Iowa City revolves around the success of the Iowa Hawkeye athletic teams, but the university also is home to the prestigious Iowa Writers Workshop, as well as the Hancher Center, used for the performing arts.

Our West High girls' volleyball had never had a winning season when I came aboard, but with the help of Maurice Batie, my assistant coach, we eventually fielded some competitive teams and qualified for the state tournament in 1991, 1992 and 1994.

The commitment level to be a successful varsity program in our conference involves more than just showing up for practice in August and relaxing when the season ends at the state tournament in November. Club season starts the week after the regular season is over, with two practices a week and tournaments on the weekends – usually on Sundays. When the club season concludes in June, the athletes come in for open gym practice sessions twice a week, and weight lifting three times per week until August. This isn't exclusive to volleyball, that's the norm for all high school sports today. It's a tremendous commitment for the athletes and the coaches to try to fit sports in with learning and teaching, family, and friends.

Coaching a girl's varsity team in this conference is time consuming. I had resigned from that job after thirteen seasons when the toll of running a competitive program had begun to skew my perspective on what athletics should be about. I'd gotten mired in expecting my teams to be better than they could be, and to be perfect on the court. When they weren't, I was too tough on them and too tough on myself. What had made me want to get into athletics in the first place – the fun, the shared goals and sense of camaraderie – had seemed a distant memory. But after some persuasion from the parents and players, I was back after a hiatus, and loving it.

Coaches can change players, but players can change coaches too.

My life changed forever when Caroline Found came onto my team.

**\*\*\*\***

Setting in volleyball is a position of glory, but it also involves tremendous pressure and responsibility. A setter is very similar to a football quarterback. In seconds, a setter has to read the opponent's defense and determine which of her hitters has the best opportunity to successfully finish the point. Setters must consistently put the ball in the best place for their hitters, and be able to remember countless play options. Most importantly, I need the setter to see the same things during the match that I see and make the correct decisions. She needs to be an extension of me.

Caroline Found, also known as Line, has been around West High volleyball since her older sister Catharine was a 6' 1" right-side hitter for West High. In 2007, when Catharine was going into her senior year, Line often tagged along with her to our open gyms. Knowing Caroline as I do now, it isn't surprising that as an eighth grader she had the confidence and audacity to ask me if she could participate in drills designed for varsity players. Handing me volleyballs as I ran repetitive passing drills, Caroline would constantly make comments like, "If you let me jump in with that group, I think I could pass as well as they do," or, "how about giving me a chance to work on my free ball passing?" I probably wouldn't have let any other younger sister of a team member do that, but I found it impossible to refuse Caroline, and eventually I'd give in to her insistent begging. Undaunted that she wasn't as skilled as the older girls, Line laughed when she made a mistake, but she clenched her jaw too. I could tell that her mistakes made her even more determined to prove to herself and others that she should be on the court.

During the fall of her eighth grade year, Caroline occasionally rode the bus with us to Saturday tournaments. She sat on the bench next to me during matches, absorbed in the action on the court and yelling loudly whenever Catharine made a good play. She kept serving-statistics on a clipboard and peppered me with questions about game strategy and why I called certain plays. Sometimes I was annoyed by her interruptions, but I generally enjoyed her passion and excitement about the sport.

We all took it for granted that Line would play on the West girls' volleyball team when she was old enough. One Saturday afternoon on the bus ride home from a tournament in Cedar Rapids, I turned around in my cramped seat. Line was sitting behind me, nodding her head to the beat of some song that only she could hear. I motioned for her to take out her ear buds.

"Caroline, you have all the qualities it takes to be a great setter: You're vocal, you're intelligent, and you're athletic. Would you like to start training as a setter next summer?"

I usually try to identify our varsity setters when they're in seventh or eighth grade, so we can work with them for several years to groom them for the position. I'd been mulling this idea of Line being a setter for some time, even though I knew she was currently a hitter on her junior-high and club teams and that her spontaneity and craziness would probably conflict with my sense of a leader's role. One time, Kelley Fliehler invited several friends, including Caroline, over for a sleepover and they began watching scary movies. During a food break, Line took the opportunity to put on a ski mask, seize a large knife and began chasing her friends while yelling "I'm going to kill you" in a perfect imitation of one of the scenes they had just watched. Their screams only fueled her determination to continue the shenanigans.

Despite her outrageousness, I loved her outgoing personality and her competitiveness. In my opinion, the setter is the most important person on the court and I didn't make this decision without a great deal of thought. In past years, kids jumped at the opportunity to be a setter.

She looked me in the eye and only hesitated for a moment. "No, I don't think so. I'm going to wear number nine like Catharine, and be an outside hitter."

For the next couple of minutes, I tried to convince her that my offer to train her as a setter was a great opportunity and that she'd be a natural in the position. But she was adamant about following in her sister's footsteps. Frustrated, I turned back around to face the front of the bus. I couldn't believe an eighth grader would blow off my suggestion.

I didn't think Caroline was tall enough to succeed in the front court. *Okay, Caroline Found*, I thought. *Let's just see how your career goes as a hitter.*

****

In an early June practice before her freshman year, Caroline tugged on my arm as we went up the steps to the weight room after an open gym.

"Brez, I'm ready to become a setter."

She'd finally realized that at 5-foot-9 she was too short to play front court for us. I got to the top of the stairwell and leaned against the open weight room door. As I looked at her earnest ocean-blue eyes searching mine inquisitively, I crossed my arms in front of my chest, and shook my head. I couldn't believe that she made this request after turning me down on that bus last fall.

"No, Caroline. You had your opportunity but you didn't take it. It's too late."

I walked into the weight room, leaving her standing on the balcony above our gym. The relationship between a setter and a coach is a special one, I thought, and if Caroline didn't accept my suggestion that she train to be a setter, there's no way I would trust her with the responsibility of running the team now. I understood that she wanted to be just like her sister Catharine and that she was only an eighth-grader last year when I offered to start training her to be a setter, but my ego was hurt when she didn't accept the invitation when it was offered.

She appeared dejected lifting weights—not cracking jokes like she normally did. I decided to ignore her. I wasn't giving in to the whims of a ninth grader who had decided to start setter training on her own time-table.

Over the course of the summer, though, she kept pestering me to participate in the setting drills during open gyms. I kept telling her "no," even though I knew, deep down, that eventually I was going to swallow my pride and give in. I knew that Caroline was a natural fit for the setter position. Not only because of the qualities I saw in her at a young age—enthusiasm, athleticism, intelligence—but because she was emerging as a leader. She had an aura about her that drew people in. The older athletes already listened when she offered suggestions during drills on the practice court. Once I saw her tell two seniors that if they could serve with more consistency, the drill would finish more quickly. They just smiled at her impudence, but she didn't seem to mind. She was compassionate and genuinely cared about others, pulling an athlete aside for reassurance when they made a mistake during practice, or running to the training room to grab an ice bag if a player turned an ankle. I knew that off the court she was the person everyone came to when they were struggling emotionally. She always knew exactly the right thing to say to help someone solve a boyfriend problem or deal with something upsetting. I needed Caroline Found on the court and she wasn't going to be there as a hitter—I needed her as my setter.

At the end of that summer in 2008, I watched her warming up with another player before the start of practice. "Liner, come over here for a second," I yelled.

She jogged over and nervously bit her thumbnail, waiting for me to tell her why she was in trouble this time.

"Are you ready to start working on your setting skills?"

Her blue eyes widened and she screamed, "What? Are you serious?!"

Before I could answer, she grabbed me in a bear hug and lifted me off the floor. Other than a couple of my defensive players, I'm easily four to six inches shorter than any of them.

"Put me down, you idiot!"

She released her grip and I dropped to the floor. She jumped up and down with the exuberance of an eight-week-old Labrador puppy with a new chew toy.

"Line, this is going to take a tremendous amount of work and dedication. I need you to promise that you're going to put your heart and soul into becoming a setter. That means not screwing around for attention and staying focused on the court."

"Brez, I promise. You're never going to regret this decision." She gave me one more bear hug, then ran back onto the court to share the news with her friends.

Caroline was a quick learner and it didn't take long for her to pick up the basics of setting. She was athletic enough to get to bad passes and she had great hands, but she was a long way off from being a setter when the start of the season rolled around at the beginning of August 2008. I decided to move her up to the sophomore team. She wasn't ready to be a full-time setter for our sophs, but on the sophomore team she'd get to play at a higher level than she would on the freshman squad.

Occasionally I went to the back gym to watch the sophomores practice and Line was usually messing around. Despite her promise that she would be focused, Line's personality wasn't going to change because she was a setter. Once I watched her take a couple of balls out of the cart and throw them at her teammates every time our sophomore coach, Kelsi Nace, had her back turned. Even if Kelsi had caught Caroline in "the act," I'm sure Kelsi would have just smiled and told her to knock it off.

One day I pulled Kelsi aside and said, "I'm just not sure this is going to work, Kelsi. Line goofs around too much, she doesn't stay focused on the court, and I just can't see her running a varsity team."

"No, Brez. I think you're wrong," Kelsi said. "She's getting so much more mature than she used to be. I think she'll surprise you."

I glanced over her shoulder. Caroline was on the floor, doing the army crawl into the other gym. I shook my head, turned away, and muttered, "More mature indeed."

****

The summer before Caroline's junior year of high school, she worked tremendously hard to master the nuances of setting. She hit every open gym; she spent extra time with me learning the plays; she easily put in three to four more hours than every other player, every week. The weekend before the varsity season starts, we attended a team camp at Central College in Pella, Iowa. We were playing Cedar Rapids Kennedy, one of our conference opponents. We were winning the match, but our timing was off and the girls weren't playing as aggressively as they normally would have done. All our hitters were returning starters and strong players, but we had a new setter, Caroline. So it was a whole new ballgame for the team.

Caroline was doing a great job managing the team; she'd been utilizing all her hitters and running a variety of play sets – until now. I watched as the defense sent her a perfect pass during one long rally. She transitioned to the net and did a nice job positioning herself under the ball. She brought her hands up to push the ball out to a hitter and then, inexplicably, *she catches the ball.* I couldn't believe it.

"What are you doing?" I yelled.

She grinned and called back to me, "I wasn't sure who to set to."

I shook my head in disbelief and turned to Scott, my assistant coach. *"Are you kidding me?"*

Caroline's teammates were all laughing hysterically. Scott was hiding a smile behind his hand, and I got even angrier. He turned to me. "Get used to it. With Line setting, you have to expect the unexpected."

During the entire two-hour drive back to Iowa City, I kept wondering if I made the right decision. We were about to start our preseason practices in two days, and I still didn't know if Caroline was capable of leading our team, but she was our best setter option. Caroline's setting was inconsistent at times, but she continued to inspire confidence in her teammates. On September 21st, we traveled to Marion to play 10th ranked Linn Mar. It was the first competition of the season for our all-state hitter, Alli O'Deen, who had been out for six months after tearing the ACL in her knee. Watching warm-ups, I could tell Alli was nervous about competing for the first time since her surgery. She was tentative on her spike approaches and grimaced every time she landed after a jump. I started to walk over to try to reassure her, but Line beat me to it.

Caroline pulled Alli close to her and I heard her say, "Alli, I'm going to set every ball to you tonight. You are going to be amazing." Alli's face lit up like a child's face on Christmas morning. Later, Alli would tell me that in that moment she knew she could succeed in volleyball again because Line had such confidence in her. We ended up sweeping the match against Linn Mar that night behind Alli's sixteen kills.

At the twenty-seven-team Westside tournament in Cedar Rapids on October 8th, 2010, Caroline finally came into her own as a setter. Playing Tripoli, the eventual 1A state champion, Line took over the match when the score was tied 8 – 8 in the first game. Taking a perfect free-ball pass from Katie Kelley our libero (a designated defensive player who can replace any other player in the back row and never leave the game) Caroline rose up, and we all thought she was going to send a quick, fast set to hard-charging Lexi Potter. Lexi jumped in the air, anticipating the set, but Line deftly dumped the ball over the net, where it fell untouched to the floor between three Tripoli players. This was the type of play that an elite, experienced setter would make. With her teammates congratulating her and patting her on the back, Caroline turned to our bench and gave us a quick smile. On the very next play, Line solo-blocked Tripoli's top hitter, despite being six inches shorter than the other girl. I could tell by the big grin on her face that she had finally gained as much confidence in her abilities as she inspired in the players around her.

Caroline was ready to put the team on her shoulders when necessary. She had become a setter.

## CHAPTER 2

# A STATE CHAMPIONSHIP

It's mid-November, and I'm nervously pacing in front of our team bench at the US Cellular Center in Cedar Rapids, IA. We're in game three of the 2010 4A Iowa state championship volleyball match.

*"Focus!"* I yell to the players on the court. We've already won the first two games, (called "sets," in volleyball) in the best-of-five series, and have a comfortable 22-16 advantage in the third. The players on the sideline begin to jump up and down with excitement. The players on the court, led by an exuberant Caroline, are laughing and bouncing up and down with anticipation.

I'm concerned. In volleyball, momentum can switch on a dime. Ankeny High School is the two-time defending state champions, and had defeated us the previous season in the championship match. I don't want this to be one of those matches that everyone talks about later: "West High had the match won, but all of a sudden Ankeny stormed back to take the third set and won the state title in five." I've seen it happen before.

"Caroline, get your team refocused," I yell again.

Someone grabs my right arm and pulls me back onto the bench. Scott is sitting there with a big smile on his face. "Sit down next to me and enjoy these last three points."

I realize, of course, that he's right. I take a deep breath and sit down on the padded seat to enjoy the moment. I look around the arena: hundreds of West High students, families and supporters are jumping up and down in their seats, the Ankeny players have a look of defeat on their faces, and my two assistant coaches, Scott and Ashten Stelken, are grinning like Cheshire cats.

On match point, Ankeny's final spike attempt feebly hits the net and falls harmlessly on their side of the floor. Every player on the court looks up at the official and when he raises his right hand to signal a point for our side of the court, the match is over. We've won our first state championship. My senior all-state outside hitter, Alli O'Deen, pumps both her arms and leans backward in utter joy, Caroline drops to her knees, and our players on the bench rush to the middle of the court. The girls pile on top of each other on the floor with the exhilaration that only a state championship can elicit.

Scott grabs me and twirls me in a circle, my feet dangling off the floor. I push him away. "Stop it! Let's act like we've been here before," I say with a smile.

As soon as the perfunctory handshake at the net with the Ankeny players and staff is complete, I run to the stands behind our bench. My parents and my aunt, Delores Bonney, are on their feet applauding with tears streaming down their faces; they know how long it's taken me to get this elusive state title. I'm in the twilight of my career. I didn't think I would ever experience this moment, and I want to share the moment with them. We hug for several minutes before I run back to join my team on the court. We pose for the state championship pictures and then gather in the foyer to meet with our families and supporters. Everyone takes turns holding the trophy as hundreds of pictures are taken. I grab my good friend Pat Smith and hand my phone to Amy Infelt, one of our parents. "Come on P, let's get a picture with the trophy." It feels so great to be holding a trophy that says "State Champions."

I can't get the smile off my face, even after Amy's finished snapping several pictures with my phone. This feels so amazing. Alli O'Deen grabs the trophy from my arms and quickly joins the other seniors so they can have a group picture. I make my way through the celebrants and step outside the venue. I lean against the outside wall and pull in a deep breath of the brisk November air. Taking a moment to enjoy the silence and the victory, I quickly scrolled through the gallery of pictures to look at the ones that Amy took of Pat and me. I enlarge each of the photos and can't believe my eyes; each frame has Caroline in the background making faces or flipping off the camera.

*"Caroline!"* I scream. I turn around and look for my impulsive setter, but she's nowhere to be found. We're going to be leaving soon and these are the only pictures I'll have on my camera – she's ruined every one of them. I vow to myself that she'll hear from me about this most recent transgression when I get the opportunity.

We head home an hour after the match is over and the bus ride is loud and raucous. It's fun to watch our girls celebrate our school's first volleyball state championship. When we arrive at school, we walk into the small auditorium, the Little Theater, for a celebratory reception with our families and friends. Alli, Katie Kelley, and Lexi Potter, the three senior captains, go to the podium and take turns talking about the season and thanking our fans for their support. After our principal, Dr. Jerry Arganbright, and athletic director, Marv Reiland, extend their congratulations, Ellyn Found, Caroline's mother approaches the stage. Ellyn's brown, shoulder-length hair frames her angular face as her tall, athletic body moves easily up the steps.

"Congratulations girls and coaches, this has truly been an amazing season. We would like to invite all you players and coaches and fans..."

"Everyone!" Line interrupts. Everybody laughs at Line's exuberance except me; I'm still miffed she ruined my pictures.

Ellyn smiles. "Yes, we'd like to invite everyone out to the farm tonight for a dance and bonfire."

The reception ends and Scott suggests that the coaches meet ahead of time at our favorite pub, Carl and Ernie's, to grab a bite to eat. We agree to meet in thirty minutes and I drive home.

Quickly pulling into my garage, I run into the house yelling, "Charlie we did it!" I begin to dance around in my living room and my long-haired best friend jumps around beside me in reaction to my ecstasy. A state championship! I've always wondered what other coaches felt after they won and now I know: total exhilaration. I also feel a sense of relief, because I would have always felt my coaching career was unfulfilled if I hadn't experienced a state title.

"Come on, buddy, let's go for a ride." Every dog owner in the world knows that 'ride' is a magic word for any mutt. Charlie, like everyone else in the community, is welcome at the Found's. It had been a gathering place for Gregg's and Catharine's friends (Caroline's older brother and sister) when they were in high school, and now serves as one for Caroline and her buddies. The ten acre farm is a favorite teen option for youth meetings, sleep-overs and simply hanging out. There's no way I'm going to leave Charlie at home to miss all the fun. The evening temperatures hover around sixty degrees, so I know he'll be all right in the car for the short time we're eating at the pub.

My assistant coaches, Scott and Ashten, Scott's wife Sheena, and my friends Pat Smith and Barb Kelley, are already at the pub when I arrive. I set the championship trophy in the middle of the table and we raise our glasses and toast a great season, several times over. It's so satisfying to be able to share this moment with the people who've supported me through the good times and the bad.

While we're eating, I get several texts from Caroline demanding to know where we are and when we're going to get to the farm. Teasing her the way she teases me, I keep telling her that we may not make it out at all. I can tell she's getting angry with our delay, because her last two texts contain all capital letters and she's added a row of questions marks. I'm not in any rush to go to the farm and join the huge throng of people that I know are already celebrating. Besides, I'm still a little miffed that Caroline ruined my pictures this afternoon when she stood behind Pat and me and flipped off the camera. As far as I'm concerned, she can just stew for a while, because I'm going to relax and enjoy this meal with my friends. When we finish our burgers, I send Caroline a text to let her know we're on our way. I smile when I read her response, "It's ABOUT time!"

Ernie and Ellyn's farm sits in the middle of rolling cornfields on a gravel road two miles outside the city limits. The large white farm house would be a perfect setting for a Grant Wood painting. The two-story, Victorian-style house is dwarfed by towering oak trees and majestic pines, and features an in-ground pool in the back yard and a large red barn off to the side of the driveway.

Ernie has renovated the barn into a teenager's playground. One half of the main floor is partitioned with drywall and has a foosball and billiards table, as well as a seating area with sofas. The old hayloft, tucked under the rafters, has been converted into a basketball court. A regulation-height hoop is attached to the barn wall and an eight-foot hoop, perfect for dunking, is off to one side. St. Louis Cardinals sports memorabilia is prominently displayed everywhere. The most exciting feature in the barn is the twenty-five foot rope swing. Riders, sitting on a twelve-inch wooden board, push off the second story loft and swing across the barn in an attempt to slap a bell hanging from the ceiling above the large entrance. It's an exhilarating ride and everyone, young and old, enjoys the challenge.

There are hundreds of cars at the farm when Charlie and I arrive. I open the car door and he sprints off to play with Lucy and Louie, the Founds' dogs. I'm as excited to celebrate with my players, their parents, and our supporters. I grab the trophy from the passenger seat and walk up the gravel lane, but then I hesitate. I can't decide whether to join the parents at the bonfire, or the celebrating kids in the barn. Through the darkness, I recognize Scott, Ashten and my friends already sitting by the roaring fire, but the sounds of laughter and a loud thumping bass pulls me towards the barn.

From the doorway, I can see someone arcing across the barn on the wooden swing and a dozen other kids surrounding the pool and foosball tables. The pounding of dancing feet in the wooden loft tells me that most of the kids are upstairs. I hurry up the steps, anxious to see my players. As soon as I reach the top step, Caroline yells out my name and runs over and gives me a monstrous hug, then just as quickly, she grabs the trophy and runs back to the middle of the dancers. She holds the trophy above her head and the rest of the team surrounds her, gyrating wildly to the song, "I Got a Feeling" by Black-Eyed Peas. I'm happy to stand on the side, but soon Shelly yells for me to join the celebration. Their youthful enthusiasm is contagious, and I jump in and make a fool of myself trying to keep up with them. Dancing has never been my forte and I'm totally out of my element.

After fifteen minutes, I know I've embarrassed myself enough and head out towards the bonfire. Parents and supporters enthusiastically yell out congratulations or high-five me as I walk past; it feels like this huge grin is permanently plastered on my face. A few people are sitting on the bales that encircle the fire, but I move to the far side, away from them, and sit down on the prickly straw.

With my elbows propped on my thighs, I rest my head on my hands, mesmerized by the glowing embers. Charlie quickly joins me and pushes his body against mine. I absentmindedly rub his ears, content to simply sit quietly and reflect on the excitement of this season. It's so satisfying to finally reach the pinnacle of high school athletics. I'm enjoying the moment, but I can't help looking ahead already to next season. Three of our elite athletes are graduating and will be playing at the next level: O'Deen is going to the University of Iowa, Kelley to Maryland and Potter to Wingate University, but we'll have a strong core of returning players and we should be a legitimate contender for another state title.

Charlie's tail begins to thump at the same time a hand pushes my shoulder.

"Move over and quit hogging the entire bale."

I smile and move to one side to make room for Caroline to sit beside me. Her blond hair, still pulled back into a ponytail, is damp with perspiration.

"After seeing you dance, I can understand why you left the barn, but are you *so old* that you need to rest?" she says with an impish grin.

"Heck, Line, I can dance circles around you. I just didn't want to embarrass you in front of your friends."

She puts her arm over my shoulder and leans in toward me. "Coach, thanks for everything and thanks for making me the setter that I am."

Without waiting for my response, she jumps off the bale and yells loud enough for everyone in the area to hear: "Hey, old lady, I think you probably should rest up before next season, because I just made a promise to everyone that we'll win another state championship!"

I shake my head and smile as she pulls a bottled water from an ice cooler and jogs towards the barn. I'm uncertain what next season will bring in terms of wins and losses, but with Caroline Found on the team, I know our season will be fun.

# CHAPTER 3
# BE A LEADER

"**B**rez, I kind of got into a little bit of trouble."
It's the first week of March in 2011, and my junior setter has stopped me in the commons near the main entrance to our school. It's been four months since we won that state championship and the euphoria still hasn't ebbed for me or the players, especially Caroline. When the clock hit midnight on New Year's Day, she sent me a text that said, *"Guess what! Only 219 days until volleyball starts!!!"* I laughed out loud when I read that, but I'm not laughing now.

"What did you do, Line?"

"We had a substitute teacher in Language Arts, and I was messing around during a test and got in trouble. She sent me to the office and I have an in-school suspension tomorrow. I'm really sorry." She looks dejected, and I can tell by the expression in her eyes that she fully expects me to be angry.

I've always stressed to our players that their behavior both on and off the court reflects on the entire volleyball program. I want them to set their standards higher than the rest of the student body, whether with academics, sportsmanship, or how they dress and act. Caroline knew I wouldn't be happy that one of my players had received an in-school suspension – particularly her, my newly named captain.

"Line, I'm extremely disappointed. However, I truly appreciate the fact that you came and told me what happened."

Relieved that I didn't yell at her, Caroline quickly replies, "I know. And I promise nothing like this will ever happen again. I already apologized to the substitute teacher."

As I walk down the hall to my third period class, it occurs to me how much she's matured in the past year. I'm actually proud of her because she came and told me what happened.

****

It's the next afternoon and I'm straightening up my classroom before heading home. I'm exhausted. It was a long, cold winter and I can't wait for our spring break, which is only a couple of days away. The thought of spending five of those vacation days in New Orleans brings a smile to my face. I can't wait to enjoy the Cajun cuisine and soak up the sun. I'm startled by a knock on the door.

I look up and see Brian Sauser, our dean of students, walking in. "Sorry to bother you, Brez, but I need to tell you what Caroline Found did today."

My great mood vanishes and my blood pressure rises.

"When she was serving her in-school suspension with two other guys, she had pizza delivered to the room. It's not necessarily against school regulations, but no one has ever done that before. I'm not happy about it."

I apologize and assure Brian that I'll talk to Caroline about appropriate behavior. Furious, I pull out my cell phone after he leaves: "Line, meet me first period tomorrow in my classroom. *DON'T BE LATE!"*

The next morning Caroline walks into my room promptly at 8:00. The big smile on her face evaporates when she sees my expression. Last night at home, all I could think about was my unpredictable setter. How can I get Line to understand her role as a captain and all it entails? I don't want to squelch her spontaneity and enthusiasm, but I also need her to think about the consequences of her actions before she acts. The pizza wouldn't be that big of a deal if it had been an isolated incident, but it wasn't. She always bends the rules, even if she doesn't actually break them. In society, some conformity is required to maintain social order; the same is true in team sports. I found out since I talked to her yesterday that her detention wasn't just for messing around, like she told me afterwards. It was because she was using her pencil to tap on her desk the answers to a quiz to assist two football players who would have flunked otherwise. Even though she was essentially trying to help two guys who needed it, she was still cheating.

"Line, have a seat."

Caroline plops down in one of the student desks, and I sit down in the chair next to her.

"About this pizza incident yesterday." She starts to interrupt me but I raise my hand to stop her. "Caroline, you have got to start using better judgment. By ordering that pizza, you made a joke of the punishment you got for cheating. You should have simply served your detention like everybody else. You can't always be the center of attention. Your actions reflect on the rest of your team."

Caroline always wants to please everyone, and I can tell by her downcast eyes that I've hurt her feelings.

"I'm going to get you a wrist bracelet with the initials WIBFW to help remind you to do *What is Best for West.*"

"What?" she replies defensively. "Brez, I never drink. I never go to parties. I never break team rules!"

"This wasn't the first time," I say.

"What else did I do?"

I can't believe she would even ask for more examples. I take a deep breath. "Caroline, what about the Parade of Champions two weeks ago?"

Each year at the girls' state basketball tournament, the Iowa Girl's High School Athletic Association (IGHSAU) hosts the state champions in every sport for the Parade of Champions. At halftime of the final game in the tournament, the winning teams walk out onto the court one by one, the first person carrying a sign with the school name at chest level. It's a very solemn affair and strictly regulated; the team members have to come out, going from the shortest to tallest person, and officials stand at various spots on the basketball floor so the girls know exactly where to turn.

Last week, when it was time for the Parade of Champions, Caroline barely got to Des Moines on time because she was playing in a club volleyball tournament two hours away in Omaha. Her dad, Ernie, got her to the arena with only minutes to spare, and she joined our team as we marched out onto the floor. I couldn't see her in the line, but when I got home that night I watched the television replay: Caroline was *skipping across the floor* and waving to the crowd.

She looked at me now and said, "I was excited to be there. There's nothing wrong with skipping. Give me another example."

"Line, you're the setter on our team and people follow your lead. It's important that you set a good example. What about the Icy Hot incident?"

When we were traveling home from the regional finals last year, the quiet of our bus ride was interrupted by someone's ungodly screams. I hurried to the back of the bus. Caroline and Shelly were jumping around in obvious pain, yelling and grabbing between their legs. No one would tell me what was going on. Finally a sophomore player told me Caroline had decided to find out what it would feel like to spread Icy Hot, a topical heat rub, in her pubic area and convinced Shelly to do it as well. It was so outrageous and over the top, I could hardly believe it. Disgusted, I had walked back to my seat in the front of the bus.

Line blushes when I bring up the Icy Hot now.

"Line," I say, "I love you to death, but you need to put the team first. That's all I'm asking."

She nods and says she'll try.

I watch her stand up and cross the floor, her face forward, shoulders back, and straw-colored ponytail bouncing. I smile as she exits my classroom – there's no way Line will ever completely conform. She reminds me of a promising young racehorse that's too spirited and occasionally bucks off its rider. My job is to harness her energy without breaking her spirit. I also think of how, despite all her zaniness, Caroline is one of the kindest people I've ever known. She wants to make other people happy. She wants to make them laugh. And most importantly, she reaches out and helps people in need. I've seen her in the cafeteria buying food for students that had either forgotten their lunches, or couldn't afford the $2.50 price tag. She wants everyone to have at least one good friend, and she's willing to be that friend to anyone who feels friendless. I love the kid to death, but she sure can drive me crazy at times like these.

I log off from my computer, pack up my briefcase, and head for home.

## CHAPTER 4

# THE UNEXPECTED

I'm sitting in my classroom, during my prep period, immersed in grading papers. It's the Monday after Easter and a beautiful spring morning. I can't help but gaze longingly out the window. My reverie is broken when my door is violently thrown open, banging into the wall. I look up. Line bursts through the doorway and heads towards my desk. I look at her ashen face and can immediately tell she's terribly shaken. Caroline can be dramatic at times, but I know from one look at her that that's not what's going on now. Something is horribly wrong.

"Brez, I have to tell you something. My mom has been diagnosed with stage four pancreatic cancer." She grabs me by the shoulders. "Everybody says she's going to be fine," she says. "Be honest with me. What are her chances?"

I don't know much about pancreatic cancer, but I do know that a stage four diagnosis is as bad as it gets. My brain can't process what she's just told me. Ellyn's the picture of health; she walks every morning and takes exceptionally good care of herself. How can she be sick? I just talked to her earlier in the week about being the parent representative for our team this fall. If what Caroline says is true, it's not only a tragedy for the Founds, but for my players as well. Ellyn is a second mother to most of our juniors.

Caroline's fingers dig desperately into my shoulders and the pain snaps me back to the present. My heart lurches. Caroline's eyes probe mine. She's desperate for reassurance and hope. *Oh my God, all I want to do is tell her everything will be okay and magically make things right in her world.*

There are times in our lives when we lie in order to protect our kids from life's harsh realities, but I know this isn't one of them. I try to hold back my tears. The lump in my throat makes it almost impossible to speak. "Line, it's not good," I say. "This is a very tough cancer to survive and a horrible diagnosis. But if anyone can overcome the odds, it's your mother."

We talk about treatment and the difficult road ahead. As the youngest of three children, Line is the only child at home, and I know this is going to be especially hard on her.

"We're here for you, kiddo, no matter what. Call me anytime, day or night, if you need to talk. Come see me whenever you need to." I give her a huge hug and she begins to sob in my arms. "Line, it's going to be okay. Your mom will beat this." But in my heart, I know that our lives are about to change forever.

Within days everyone in our small community has heard the terrible news, and it's hard to fathom how this horrible disease could strike the all-American family: Ernie, a prominent orthopedic surgeon, Gregg, an NBA research analyst for ESPN, Catharine, a starting front court player for Trinity College, Caroline, the love of everyone's life, and Ellyn, the Leave it to Beaver mother.

Like everyone else, I'm devastated. I haven't had many conversations with Ernie because he's generally the silent supporter standing in the corner of the gym, but Ellyn has always been around West High volleyball as a parent representative and to help out with team meals and player bonding activities. As outgoing as this family is, Ernie and Ellyn keep their personal things pretty tight to the vest. I'm unsure of how to even approach Ellyn. I want to let her know she's in my thoughts and prayers, and ask if there's anything I can do to help, but

I don't have a close enough relationship with her to call. I would feel like I was intruding at a very private time.

Finally I decide to send her an email. I let her know that the team would like to supply her family with a month of prepared food from Naomi's Kitchen, a local caterer. I thought this might be a perfect option so that Ellyn wouldn't have to worry about making meals for her daughter and husband. She simply had to select the quantity and type of food that sounded appealing, and the food just has to be un-thawed for suppers. I attach Naomi's menu and I extend my prayers, support, and love.

The next day I get a reply from Ellyn thanking me for my note of encouragement. She said it's been overwhelming to go from seemingly picture-perfect health to being diagnosed with a terminal illness. It was obvious from her note that many people in the community were reaching out to her and her family but that at this time, she needed privacy to process this devastating news. She asked me to continue praying for her mental and physical strength and her family's. Then she had one final request:

*I know you and Caroline have a very special relationship, and I know she will need you through thick and thin, even when you would like to choke her. She has grown up in many ways these past few weeks, yet I can't imagine what this is like for a 16-year-old girl. Thank you for all you do for her. Thank you, Brez. I am trying hard to believe each day.*

I reread the paragraph about Caroline and my tears begin to fall. I know that we're all going to have to support and protect Line as much as possible. Ellyn, always gracious, appreciative and polite, is more concerned about her daughter's welfare than her own impending journey.

## CHAPTER 5

# OPEN GYM

The humid June air is stifling. We haven't even started our weekly open gym session and the players' shirts are drenched in sweat. My girls are sitting around in small groups but everyone is strangely subdued. I finally figure out the problem; everyone is anxiously awaiting Line's entrance to the gymnasium. Caroline is the energy that we all feed off, and she's late because she's still at softball practice.

"Let's get started. Three-minute jog and then partner ball-handling," I tell them.

The players finish putting on their court shoes and start jogging slowly around the gym in groups of two and three. Then suddenly the gym is filled with loud, raucous music pouring from the portable speaker system on the other side of the gym. I don't even need to turn around to know that Line has arrived. The jogging players smile because they know what's going to happen next. "Line, turn down that music!" I bellow. Caroline turns the music down one notch, but it's still only a few decibels below that of a fighter jet at takeoff. She saunters over, giving me an impish grin.

"How's it going, kiddo?" I ask.

"It's all good. Mom's doing well. Hey, will you buy one of these from me?" Caroline pulls a deep purple t-shirt from her duffel bag. "Team Ellyn" is printed in bold block letters on the front. "We're going to have a 'Beat Cancer' softball game next week and everyone is wearing these to the game."

"Of course I will, gladly," I say. I look down as she pulls on her volleyball shoes and I immediately choke up. Caroline has painted "ELLYN FOUND" on one of her shoes and "FIGHT 4 MOMMA" on the other. I turn away so she doesn't see the tears welling in my eyes.

"Get out there and join your team, you're already late," I say gruffly. She skips off to join the others, who have finished jogging and are on the floor doing their stretches. I'm struck by the enormity of the pressure that she's under. I know that she feels she has to maintain a façade of normalcy, even though her life has been rocked upside down. I wonder how long she'll be able to maintain her composure. I remember the text she sent me at 12:01 am on January 1st in anticipation of the upcoming season, but this isn't the senior year she expected six months earlier.

I watch her closely during the entire practice. She isn't playing well; her sets to the hitters are poor, the hitters' timing is off, and the team struggles as a result. She encourages and pushes her teammates during the drills, but her emotions seem forced. She looks like she has lost weight and her facial features are drawn and gaunt. She looks tired.

"We're not looking like the defending state champs right now," I mutter to Scott when he joins me along the net. He looks at me and nods grimly.

The girls finish up on the court. They tear down the nets and put all the equipment away. We huddle up as we do at the end of every practice.

"Not our best effort today," I say. "Let's make sure at our next open gym that we bring the right energy." They nod in agreement. They understand the amount of work it takes to hold onto a state championship trophy.

"Hey, pool party today at Laynie's house!" Caroline announces in a vintage Line moment. Laynie Whitehead is a freshman, this is her first year on varsity and this is one of her first open gyms, and now Caroline just invited eighteen kids to swim at her house, even though the

Founds have a pool of their own. If Laynie is shocked, she doesn't show it. Like everyone always does, she goes along with Caroline's idea and agrees that everyone should go to her house and swim. I smile at Line being Line. The team quickly agrees and we put our hands together in the middle of the huddle.

We all look expectantly at Caroline, because she directs the end of our huddles. A good team captain keeps her teammates focused, but a great captain makes everyone feel important. Line is the best I've ever coached at doing this. Most teams end practices or huddles by counting to three, but Line decided that instead the number we count to should be the jersey number of a player that hustled or played well in practice. Today it was Laynie's turn to be recognized, because she graciously accepted Caroline's offer to have everyone over to her house.

"West on fourteen," Line's deep, throaty voice yells from the middle of the clustered players.

"One, Two, Three, Four, Five, Six, Seven, Eight, Nine, Ten, Eleven, Twelve, Thirteen, Fourteen, WEST," the girls shout in unison, and quickly exit the stifling gym.

I turn to Scott. "We need to talk."

We move over to the corner of the gym so we can get relief from whatever bit of breeze might come through the open doors.

I look at him. "Our job is to do what's best for the team and the program. I can't help but think ahead and wonder how Ellyn's health is going to impact the players. She's like a mother to all our seniors. If her health continues to deteriorate, there's a possibility she may not even survive to the end of the season. Furthermore," I continue, "where's Line's head going to be? She's going to be impacted by her mother's condition. We need to come up with ideas about how to support her and her family, as well as do what's best for the team. This is going to be such a difficult balancing act." I inhale deeply. It's time to face the elephant in the room. "Scott, do we need to start training another setter?"

Laynie, a precocious ninth grader, is our future setter, but she's a year away in her development. There's no way she can step in and run the team if Ellyn gets worse, or Caroline needs time away from the court. Erin Weathers, a junior, is a good setter for the junior varsity level, but I think she's too short to play front court on our varsity. The tall hitters from other teams would hit right over her outstretched arms. I feel like they, the seniors, would be critical of her setting—not because she's not capable—but because she's not Caroline. I trust and depend on Scott to give me an objective opinion. He's fair and I value his judgment.

He looks at me and says, "No, we need Line and she needs us. If Ellyn passes away during the season, God forbid, volleyball is going to be Caroline's refuge. If we start training another setter, it'll send her the wrong message. She'll interpret that as meaning we've lost hope for Ellyn. We have to stand by Line. Besides, we really don't have anyone else that can set."

I feel uneasy as I drive home. I understand and agree with Scott's assessment, but the nagging thought continues to roll around in my brain: We may be making a mistake by not using the summer to get another setter ready, just in case.

## CHAPTER 6

# TEAM CAMP

It is August 4th, and once again we're at Central College for team camp. It's hard to believe that it's only been a year since Caroline caught the ball when she was setting. A lot has happened in that time. Caroline's gradually developing into an outstanding setter, we won the state title, and Ellyn was diagnosed with cancer.

Today we look horrendous on the court. We're not playing with the focus and determination of a defending state champion. We have no energy on the court and we're getting beat by teams that we shouldn't be losing to.

I know that it's hard to be excited about playing in these conditions. The temperature is pushing one hundred degrees outside and the heat index in this non-air-conditioned building must be twenty degrees higher, but our problems are more complex than simply being hot.

Earlier this week, Caroline was with her family in New Hampshire for their annual family vacation. Ellyn's health took a turn for the worse while they were out there and she had to be hospitalized. Line got back to Iowa City just a few hours before we were to leave for camp. The girls are obviously worrying about Line, and I understand that volleyball is secondary in their thoughts. We're uninspired on the court and our play is sloppy. If we're going to salvage the season, I have to help the kids learn to block out their emotions.

I call them over after our third consecutive loss. I know it's difficult for them to maintain focus on the court, especially Caroline, but I need to get their attention and I need to get it now.

"This is not an acceptable level of play," I tell them, feigning anger. "If you do not want to be on the court, then we might as well pack our bags and head back to Iowa City. This is pathetic and quite frankly, an embarrassment for West High. You don't deserve to wear a West jersey. Go turn your shirts inside out before our next match and we'll leave them that way until we play with some enthusiasm. Winning or losing is irrelevant, but lack of effort and passion isn't!"

Their astonishment quickly turns to anger and resentment. I can tell that Anna Pashkova, our feisty libero whom we all call "The Russian," is about to tell me to go to hell. I don't blame her. I don't even like myself at this moment, but I would rather have them angry at me than angry at life. They need to understand that when they're on the court, they have to focus on the task at hand – playing volleyball – and shut out other distractions. Volleyball could end up being their emotional life-line for the upcoming season; I know that we're going to experience many trying times. Somehow these seventeen- and eighteen- year old girls will need to redirect their grief when they're on the court, and learn how to manage their anger. I realize, though, that this means that I may end up being their emotional target and the brunt of their frustration while I attempt, through any means possible, to keep them on task.

I watch them march off in defiance to a corner of the gym and turn their shirts inside out.

Scott looks at me with confusion in his eyes and I say, "No part of this season is going to be easy. I know we both just want to hug Line and shelter all of them from this situation, but we can't. We have to allow them the freedom to grieve and be there for them in any way possible, *but* when they're on the court, they're going to have to learn how to shut out all other distractions."

He nods in agreement and places his arm gently over my shoulder as we walk to the next match. I'm going to have to lean on Scott this season, a fact that makes me uncomfortable. I'm generally not someone who relies on others for emotional support, but this season the situation is different than other years. We're all going to have to step out of our comfort zone. Scott is kind and sensitive and I know I can always count on his loyalty, but I've never been comfortable reaching out to him on a personal level—I would feel too vulnerable.

We perform much better in our next match, and Caroline sidles over to me near the side of the court after we win.

"Hey, do you think we can turn our jerseys back now?" she says with an impish grin.

I pretend to ponder her request with extreme seriousness. "Yeah I suppose so, but only on a trial basis," I tell her.

"Well it's a good thing for you," she quips. "I think The Russian was going to hang you in effigy pretty soon!" She bounces away to tell the team the news.

I turn to Scott, "We have our Line back!" We both smile and head to the townhouse dorm we're renting to get changed for supper.

Most years at team camp we go out to a local Mexican restaurant in downtown Pella on Friday night, but not this time. Caroline suggests that we order in pizza from Happy Joe's so that we can relax in the living room of our townhouse and not have to dress up to go out. I thought it was a great idea and throughout the evening, Line and Shelly entertain us with jokes and loud burps—they'll do or say anything to amuse the rest of us. By the time we're done eating, my sides hurt from laughing. Even though we're having a great time, it's obvious that Caroline's good humor is forced. Her mind is elsewhere.

It doesn't take long for ten hungry volleyball players to devour six pizzas.

"Mafia!" Caroline yells and the girls quickly clear a path through the discarded pizza boxes. Scott and I join them and we all sit on the floor in a shoulder-to-shoulder circle. Mafia is a nonsensical game that has become an annual team camp tradition. Caroline, as always, is the narrator, and she makes up goofy scenarios like, "The Russian is walking down the middle of the street at midnight. A passing van hurls a rabid monkey on her back and she gets bitten and dies." The rest of the game involves guessing who the killer is, who gets saved and who dies. Most of the time I don't even know all the rules, but it does seem that Scott and I "die" at a much higher rate than any of the girls.

We take a break after an hour and make ice cream sundaes. The girls each begin to make a variety of ice cream sundaes, accessorized with everything from peanuts to hot fudge to whipped cream. Part way through our ice cream orgy, I see Caroline texting non-stop on her phone. I lean over and ask her what's going on and she says, "It's Mom. She's in the hospital in Iowa City and not doing well."

"Let's go," I whisper. "We can be back in Iowa City by midnight if we leave now."

She looks at me incredulously and says, "No, I won't do that to my team. They need me here."

I don't want to push her too hard, but I want her to know it'll be all right if she changes her mind or if things get worse for her mom. "Caroline, no matter what time it might be, please wake me and we can be back in Iowa City in less than two hours," I tell her. She looks at me, fighting back tears, and nods.

In an effort to lighten the mood, I decide to regale the team with my rendition of "Tip Toe through the Tulips" in my best Tiny Tim impression. I'm accustomed to having the kids think I'm a dork, and this time is no exception. Everyone laughs hysterically as I dance around the room. I feel pretty old when I realize that Scott is the only person in the room who's even heard of

Tiny Tim. I survive being the brunt of the girls' jokes for the next five minutes before telling them that it's time to hit the sack. We have a big day of competition tomorrow and I want my team to get some rest.

I wake up tired and sore. I hate sleeping on dorm room beds. The townhouse is great with its eight bedrooms, kitchen and lounge area, but I prefer a mattress that doesn't feel like it's stuffed with grapefruits and walnuts. I knock on Scott's door. "Hey, let's wake the munchkins and get some breakfast in them," I yell through the door.

Scott comes out with tousled hair and bags under his eyes. It doesn't look like he slept any better than I did. We walk up to the second level and knock on the first door. No response. Scott opens the door and we look inside. Both bunks are empty and the mattresses are missing. I look at Scott and we both shrug. We head to the next bedroom and knock. Once again there's no answer. One glance and it's obvious that this room's empty as well.

"I'm not sure what's going on," I tell Scott, "but I guarantee you that Line has something to do with this!"

"Without a doubt," he replies. "If we find Line, we'll find the other nine players."

We open the doors to the third and fourth bedrooms: vacant. We walk quietly to the fifth bedroom. Scott throws the door open and we both look curiously inside. There they are – all ten players slept in a room designed for two. Poor Laynie is lying on a mattress balancing precariously on the top of two dressers pushed together. She's lucky she didn't fall and break her neck. The rest are sardined into the beds and on the floor, wide awake, and giggling.

"Would any of you care to explain?" I ask, looking directly at Caroline.

"We wanted to be together!" she explains. "We don't want any of the egos like we had on the team last year. This is going to be the closest team that West High has ever had!"

Last season some of our players had developed huge egos, showing more concern about personal recognition and accolades than team success. At the time, I remember feeling it was the most difficult and stressful season I had ever been a part of in my 25 year coaching career.

I turn away from the doorway and look at Scott, "Well?" I ask him.

"I got nothing," he replies with a smile. "With Caroline's leadership this season, I think we can agree that our life's not going to be boring."

The team has breakfast, and then we walk over to the gymnasium. All the teams have been placed in new pools based on yesterday's results. We won just enough matches to be paired with the better teams at the camp.

I was hoping that we would be over our first-day jitters, but the second day of the competition is much the same as the first day. We don't win a single match and, quite honestly, to me as a coach of the state champions, it's embarrassing. We're competitive with some of the teams, but we can't close out any games and get a win.

Our final match of the day is against Iowa City High School, our cross-town rival. Caroline is playing terribly, setting balls off the court, not transitioning from offense to defense, and doing a poor job of using her hitters. Shelly, our top-returning hitter, isn't looking much better. Her hits are going out of bounds, her serves are going into the net, and she's not communicating with her teammates on the court. They're both all-state caliber players that I'm depending on to carry the load at the beginning of the season until our younger players get comfortable. They need to step up their games, but they look like first-year varsity athletes instead of returning starters.

We lose the first set to City High 16-21 and are down 2-19 in the second when I turn to Scott and say, "It's time to send a message about expectations. What I'm about to do is going to break my heart, and I won't be able to do it again the rest of the season."

Scott looks at me and says, "Whatever you need to do, I'm with you."

I promptly call time out and the players gather around me, their heads hanging low. I turn to Caroline. "Line, you're one of the elite returning setters in the state! Setters have to be leaders. *Lead this team.*" I turn to Shelly. "Shell, you're not any better! Lose the attitude and be a better teammate. Both of you have a seat on the bench. Scott, find six people who want to be on the court."

Caroline takes my criticism in stride. Setting is the most powerful and glorious position, but it also comes with the most pressure and responsibility. I need Line to know that if she's not emotionally capable of leading this team then she needs to step aside, whether it's at a practice, a drill or a game. I understand she wants to be on that court, but not at the expense of her teammates. Caroline waits until I finish talking and pulls the team in for a huddle. She extends her hand into the middle of the circle and the other nine girls follow her lead. "West on four," she yells. "Come on West. We can do this."

I know every player on the team is feeling very protective of Caroline, and I'm sure they're angry I've called her out. However, these girls are very competitive and they're intelligent enough to understand that we're only going to be successful this season if Caroline is able to focus when she's playing volleyball. As the team walks back onto the court, I repeat to Scott that I will *never* be able to do that again, no matter what. I certainly don't want to hurt Caroline's feelings. I wish I could erase her worries about her mother. But I'm also responsible for the entire team, and I need to do what's best for the whole.

I couldn't be more pleased with the heart and effort that my players exhibit during the remainder of the set. Ironically, with Caroline and Shelly on the bench, we run off seventeen straight points to tie the set 19-19 before losing 24-26. Losing this match isn't important. What matters to me is that for the first time this weekend my girls exhibit passion and effort on the court.

Months later, after the season was over, Caroline's father Ernie told me that Caroline was jumping up and down with excitement when she came home from team camp. "Dad, we're going to be awesome this year," she told him. "I'm going to help Shelly become Player of the Year in Iowa. She's going to get the best sets she's ever hit!" This was a typical reaction for Line. Even though our play was abysmal, she was still optimistic and excited.

She always believed there was a silver lining.

## CHAPTER 7
# PRESEASON PROGNOSIS

It's Wednesday, August 9th, and we've just finished our third day of preseason practice. I've had time to evaluate my players and I want to jot down my thoughts about their strengths and weaknesses, to come up with a possible starting lineup. I begin my list with the names of returning starters.

Caroline will definitely be our setter, even though I'm worried about her mental state because of her mother's health. An honorable mention all-state athlete, she's the heart and soul of our team. She's the consummate leader, instilling confidence in those around her. I depend on her to keep tabs on the pulse of the team. She squelches conflicts between teammates and comes to me with her concerns and suggestions. I love that her crazy antics keep her teammates loose during the match. She's a bit small at 5-foot-9, but does an admirable job blocking at the net, despite going up against much taller hitters. I know we're solid with Caroline setting, so that position is the least of my concerns.

Shelly is guaranteed a starting position as one of the two outside hitters. A three-sport athlete – volleyball, basketball, and softball – Shelly (Caroline calls her Sis) is 6-foot-1. She was an honorable mention all-conference last year, and she has a lightening quick arm-swing. Shelly has a great sense of humor and often conspires with Line to liven up practice. I feel she has the potential to be one of the top hitters in the state, but I'm concerned about her lack of mental toughness. There were times in the past that she had difficulty maintaining her composure after committing an error on the court. If we're going to be successful, she needs to be able to shake off mistakes. Scott and I always preach "next ball" to the players – forget the play that just happened, move onto the next. Shelly needs to embody that mantra if she's going to reach her full potential.

The last returning starter is Olivia Fairfield, our middle blocker. We have two Olivia's on the team so the girls call Olivia Fairfield "Eunice," (although I usually call her Betty, because it is an easier name to yell and have her hear me). We call the other Olivia, Olivia Mekies, "Squeaks." A senior, Eunice has the ability to dominate the net and shut down opposing hitters. She plays with a lot of heart, but is a bit undersized for a middle blocker at six feet tall. Last season she was more of a finesse hitter, sending the ball to open areas of the court. This year she's going to have to be a stronger hitter than she was in the previous season if we're going to be a contender for a state title. She has to hit balls hard enough that opposing defenses are afraid to pass for fear of getting hurt.

I'm going to have to rely on Shelly and Eunice to be our "go to" hitters early in the season. I'm a little concerned about our team dynamics, though. During the summer open gyms, I sensed there was a small rivalry going on between my two returning hitters. Shelly and Eunice's body language during hitting drills made me think they've been having a silent tug of war as to who's going to be the "big dog" on the team. Line even approached me to voice her concern about their attitudes. If there's tension between my top two hitters, it could be a recipe for disaster.

Anna Pashkova, aka "The Russian," was a defensive starter for us last season, but this year as a senior, she will step into the role as our libero. Anna is the antithesis of Line and Shelly: she's stoic, calm, and focused when she's off the court. On the volleyball court, however, she is the sparkplug and catalyst for our team. She celebrates big points louder than anyone else, and jumps four feet in the air after a particularly big point. Anna has great court sense and is able to anticipate the play before it happens. I know I can count on her to maintain her composure in pressure situations. She's a star in the making.

I look at my list:  Four of my seven positions are solid, but I still need to find three more hitters and another defensive player. Olivia (Squeaks) Mekies appears to be the front runner to anchor our back court along with Anna, which I find somewhat surprising, because I never thought Squeaks would be a varsity player. When she was a freshman and sophomore player, she visibly reacted to her errors, grabbing her hair, making faces, and getting into a funk that she couldn't get out of. I constantly urged her to do a better job of hiding her expressions. She saw only limited varsity action as a junior, but this summer she's been a pleasant surprise. She now maintains her composure and is very quick in the back court. The position will be hers as long as she shows she can handle the pressure of a match.

Hannah Infelt, another of our hitters over six foot tall, is the top contender for the other middle blocking spot. In the past she played on the right front for us, and wasn't a big part of our offense because we had two all-state hitters playing next to her, so she didn't get set as often as the others. The change to the middle of the net will involve a huge learning curve for her. She'll have to learn many new blocking assignments and adjust to hitting faster sets. I'm concerned about whether she'll be quick enough to play middle, but I know she's extremely intelligent, as her 4.0 grade point average attests. She should be a fast learner and will work hard to improve.

Two underclassmen seem to be the front-runners for the two remaining positions. Sophomore Mollie Mason will be a good role player for us on the outside. Unlike

Shelly, who plays the other outside position, Mollie is an extremely quiet young woman. Outside hitters are the most likely players to get the set on a broken play, when a bad pass pulls the setter off the net. When this happens it's important to have a dependable outside hitter to keep the ball in play. Molly doesn't have a huge swing but she has good ball control and won't hurt us by hitting the ball into the net or off the court. She's demonstrated that she has the skills to fill the role of a ball-control hitter.

Laynie Whitehead is a 6-foot-1 left-handed hitter and she puts a huge block against the other teams outside hitters. Our precocious freshman has good leadership qualities and I know she'll fit in with a senior-dominated squad. Innocent for even a freshmen, the seniors enjoy teasing her in a good-natured way, but she takes it all in stride. Laynie's untested but she's a potential Division I college player, and I'm confidant she'll remain poised under pressure.

We have enough talent that we could contend for a state title by the end of the season, but it's all going to depend on Caroline. In order for us to have consistency on offense, she needs to put our experienced hitters in a position to terminate the ball. More importantly, she must help our newcomers—Mollie and Laynie, and Hannah Infelt in their new positions—ease into their roles and gain some confidence. It's difficult to adjust to the pressure of playing the top teams in the state each week. I know we're only going to be as good as Caroline allows us to be.

# CHAPTER 8

# THE FIRST WEEK OF PRACTICE

It's Friday, August 11th, the fifth day of the preseason practices. As any volleyball coach can verify, the last day of preseason practice in Iowa is brutal. August temperatures drag everyone down and the repetitive drills become boring.

Last night, Shelly and Line called me and started screaming over the phone that they were going to call the Department of Human Services.

"What the heck are you even talking about?" I asked.

"We just googled Tiny Tim and we want you to know that this is a form of child abuse...." I couldn't help but smile as I cut off their phone call in mid-sentence. That impulsive performance at team camp had come back to haunt me.

I watch the girls practice and think the team's looking darn good. Caroline seems to be to shaking off the rust, and our hitters, particularly Shelly and Eunice, are looking like all-state-caliber players. I'm confident those two will be ready to carry the team on their shoulders offensively. Defensively, Pashkova and Squeaks simply do not let a ball touch the floor, and Hannah, Laynie and Mollie Mason are beginning to look comfortable in their new starting roles. My biggest concern is that we don't have a lot of depth. We'll be solid as long as one of my starters doesn't sustain a season-ending injury.

As we finish with warm-ups, Marv Reiland, West High's athletic director, walks into the gym to watch some of our practice, something he does several times a week. Line, warming up with Hannah, yells, "Mr. Reiland! We don't look that great right now, but you just wait, we're going to be a *better* team than last season!" Marv, a very stoic man, looks at Caroline and replies, "I hope that's true, Caroline, I hope that's true." He glances at me and smiles slightly. I'm cautiously optimistic that we might have a pretty good squad this year, but my hopes are nothing compared to Line's exuberance. Marv shakes his head and leaves the gym. I can tell he's amused by Line's excitement.

My players move to the endlines of both courts and begin serving with partners. Scott is watching the court adjacent to mine and I motion him over. During practice this week, the two of us have spent quite a bit of time talking about our starting lineup. We want to make sure we have the best-skilled players on the court during our matches. We've agreed with each other about most of the lineup, but I'm still unsettled about the status of one particular player.

"Scott, I think we need to get Kelley on the court. Do you have any ideas how we can get her in the rotation?" I ask.

Kelley Fliehler is a 5-foot-10 senior. I don't know her as well as I do some of the other players because she's fairly reserved, and last season she primarily played in the junior varsity matches. But after watching her play at team camp and this year's preseason practices, I've really started to appreciate what she brings to our team. She's always pleasant and respected by her teammates and has solid volleyball skills. She's impressed me with her work ethic each day in practice. She's not loud like Caroline or Shelly, but I notice her quietly pat her teammates' backs when they have a nice play. She has a calming presence on the court.

Scott pauses for a moment. "Well, she's not tall enough to block in the middle or right front positions. We don't have an outside hitting position open, because Mollie is doing a nice job there. Kelley's one of our best players in receiving serve, so maybe we can find a back court position for her?"

"Scott, the problem is that Squeaks is quicker and Anna is the best defensive player in the state. I just don't think there'll be many opportunities for Kelley to get playing time in the back row."

"Well, our only other option is to use her as a role player when someone is struggling or when we need a tough server."

We table our discussion and turn our attention back to the players. I know this will continue to bother me. Kelley is too good to be just a junior varsity member, but barring an injury, there doesn't seem to be a spot in the rotation for her.

We start a passing drill. Scott has half the players on one court and I have the other half on my court. In order to complete the drill, both courts must complete twenty consecutive passes without an error. After a full week of three-hour practices each day, the girls are tired and getting sloppy. In order to complete twenty passes, they're going to have to focus and communicate. If either court makes an error, the count goes back to zero and they have to start over.

After twenty minutes, the girls are still doing the same drill. Every time they've gotten close to completing the twenty perfect passes, they've mishandled a ball. My players are getting frustrated that they have to keep starting over, but the angrier they get, the worse they play. When we start the count at zero for the sixth time, Caroline yells at me from across the net, "Brez, what kind of gas does a moped use?"

I'm as frustrated as the players that we're still here. It's hot in the gym, and we should have been able to end this drill in four minutes. I'm irritated that Line would even ask me something like that. *This is a perfect example of our lack of focus and the reason we're still trying to get twenty passes in a row,* I think.

"A moped uses the kind of gas that comes from the

pump," I say without looking at her. *What an asinine question,* I think. *She doesn't even own a moped.*

It takes us fifteen more minutes to finally complete the drill. I tell the girls to take a water break. *It's ridiculous that it took that long for this drill,* I think. *Our freshman team could have gotten it done faster.* Frustrated, I head out to the water fountain for a quick drink.

We've been going hard for almost two hours, but I want to get some repetitive hitting in before we're done for the day. I come back into the gym and notice that most of the senior girls are kneeling in a semi-circle around Caroline. There are notebook-size papers on the floor, each protected with a sheet of plastic. What's so important that it's taking up our practice time? We've already been in this hot gym far too long. I walk over to the girls and see what has them so engrossed: Line's senior pictures. There are fifteen sheets of photos, with four pictures each, laid out on the gym floor; the girls are oohing and ahhing, pointing out their favorites.

Line looks up. "Brez, come see my pictures. Which ones do you like the best?"

"Caroline. They all look beautiful, but this is neither the time nor the place." I'm more than a little irked by my captain's behavior, first the moped comment and now the picture interruption. "Can't this wait until practice is over? I would love to look at them once we're done."

She gathers up the pictures and walks over to the sideline to where her gear sits in a pile against the wall. I know that her lack of concentration is partly related to her mother's failing health. I can't begin to imagine the unending stress in her life. But there's going to be a direct correlation between our team's success and her ability to focus on volleyball.

She puts the pictures in her duffle bag, then jogs back across the court, playfully punching me in the shoulder as she passes me on her way to her teammates. She begins to set balls to her hitters, and her strong athletic body moves effortlessly on the court. It's obvious that she worked hard in the weight room this summer – I've never seen her in better shape. She's going to have a tremendous senior season. I fully expect her to be voted first team all-state.

We finish the drill and everyone heads home, anxious to get out of the oppressive heat. Line and I both forget about her pictures. Looking back at this moment, I have two regrets: One that I never took time out of practice to look at all her senior pictures—I never did get to see them—and two, that I didn't ask her about the moped.

# PART II

## CHAPTER 9

# LETTERS FOR HEAVEN

At six a.m. I wake up drenched in sweat with a pounding headache. It feels like I'm hung over and I can't figure out why. Suddenly I remember: The call from last night. Caroline is dead. I've slept for an hour and a half. I was on my phone during most of the night as the horrifying news spread and people called and texted me. I finally turned the phone off at four-thirty, and went to bed for a quick nap.

I begin to cry again. I dread facing my team. What can I possibly say or do to help them? I don't think I have the emotional fortitude to even help myself right now, much less fifteen others. I can't come up with any ideas about what to do with the players when we meet in a few hours. I've texted them to meet with me and Scott at eight in the gym. I feel like we should all sit near the setter's position on the court, the exact spot where Caroline was twenty-four hours earlier. Perhaps we can sit and talk and just be there for each other. I have nothing beyond that, but I know I'm going to have to pull myself together and somehow find the strength for those girls.

I've only been in my office at school for ten minutes when Scott walks in. Neither of us says a word; we simply fall into each other's arms and sob. We stay like that for several minutes and then I pull myself back.

"What are we going to do?" I say. "Line is...no was," I correct myself, "our team. She was the spark, the one who lived to play volleyball. What are we going to do now? She was the one who enjoyed life to the fullest. This simply isn't fair. What the hell are we going to do to get through this?"

Scott pulls me into his arms again and holds me as my tears wet the front of his shirt. We stay that way until I hear the locker room door open slowly and tentatively. Kelley and Shelly walk in, looking uncertain and hesitant. Scott and I open up our arms and Kelley falls into mine and Shelly falls into Scott's. We let them cry for a good few minutes until their tears eventually slow. They extract themselves from our arms and look imploringly at us, their eyes filled with anguish and questions. There are no words to comfort them and I don't try. What the heck do I have to offer them? I can barely hold my own self together. The words *we lost Line* keep looping through my mind like a tape set on automatic replay.

We walk slowly out of my office and to the gym, all four of us clinging to each other. It's as if none of us want to return to the very court that will forever haunt us with memories of Caroline.

"Come on, we can do this. The others will be out there soon," I tell Kelley and Shelly.

I push open the double doors and we walk into the darkened gym. I have no intention of turning on the bright fluorescent lights. I want the blackness to envelope me, to blur the reality of our loss. I sense that others are present as we make our way toward the volleyball net. As my eyes adjust to the light, I'm shocked to see the entire team already assembled, even though we're not supposed to meet here for another hour. Then I become aware that we're not alone. There are groups of kids scattered throughout the gym. There must be fifty people here. I can't begin to comprehend why all these kids are here. *What are they doing? This is our time together. Besides, this many kids won't fit on Caroline's spot.*

I'm selfishly trying to protect my team and our grief,

but then it hits me: everyone lost Caroline. This is not our loss alone. Of course kids will gather at the very spot where they felt closest to Line—in the gym where she played volleyball. This is Friday, the last day of summer vacation, and they want to be with the people who will come to represent Caroline—my players.

"Hey, everyone, come on over here," I call. "Please, come and join us."

Like zombies, students start trudging toward the court. I realized I grossly underestimated the crowd; there are literally hundreds of students gathering around us. My heart aches as I see the broken-heartedness in their young eyes.

I take a deep breath. "We all loved Caroline. She was the perfect friend and the most passionate person I ever met. I know this isn't fair," I pause. "I am not the one to lead a prayer right now, but why don't we close our eyes for a few minutes and offer up the prayers in our hearts."

After a few moments, I suggest that maybe we could all share our favorite memories of Caroline. Students begin to reminisce. Some recount Line's goofy pranks and sense of humor. Others talk about how she made them feel important.

Amy Kanellis, one of our fabulous guidance counselors, walks up and sits down on the floor next to me. I'm so grateful to have another adult, besides Scott, here to help me. Amy is one of Ellyn's closest friends and had been counseling Caroline about how to manage her grief and get back in touch with her faith in God. Sorrow is etched on her face. The bags under her red eyes attest to the face that she hasn't slept either, but she maintains her composure as she tells the kids how important it is for them to take care of themselves— drink enough water, eat and sleep—and that the counselors will be available at the school if anyone needs some help.

When she finishes talking, there's complete silence. I

know these kids need something more.

"Hey, why don't we write letters to the Found family?" I finally suggest. A few kids nod, but most just stare at me with blank expressions. I go to my office and gather as many pens as possible and some white typing paper. Back in the gym Scott helps me pass out the supplies. The kids write, some not seeming to know what to say, others appear to be pouring out their hearts. When they're all finished, we gather up the sheets of paper and put them in a bag to deliver to the Founds.

I then give everyone a yellow piece of paper and say, "We have one more important letter to write. Write this letter to Caroline. Tell her how much she means to you and anything else you want to say." I watch them huddle over their yellow sheets, as if they don't want anyone else to see what they're putting down, and write purposefully and earnestly. I can tell they're telling Caroline in their own words, how much they love her.

We're in the gym about two hours, with more and more people coming in, including all the girls' parents. I'm very concerned that the kids will want to visit the crash site. The accident occurred only a few blocks from the school, and I'm worried about their safety on such a busy street. I suggest that everyone take an hour's break, and then we all meet at a spot close to the accident scene and walk down there together.

I go to the store and purchase enough flowers for my players to place at the tree, and as a result, I'm a little late arriving at the designated meeting area at the University of Iowa's soccer fields. I cannot believe my eyes when I pull up in my car; there must be two hundred people milling around, including representatives from several television stations. I know both of the television reporters. They quickly come up to me and ask for a statement. "Please just give us our time to grieve. One of us will give you a statement when we come back to our cars," I reply wearily. The reporters nod with understanding, and respectfully shoot footage of the crowd and the accident site from afar.

My players and I hold hands as we walk with the other students. Holding hands is the only comfort we can offer each other. It's only five hundred yards to the accident site, but it seems like five miles. I'm not sure where the exact spot is, but Olivia Fairfield's mom, Cathy, knows where it is and she's with us now, leading the way. As we trudge along it feels as if the air is closing in. My chest constricts and I can't breathe. When we come around a bend in the road, I'm surprised to see Iowa City police cruisers on both sides of the median. There's a row of fifteen small trees, twenty feet apart, growing in the middle of the median. The trees are only about four inches in diameter and fifteen feet tall. Next to the third tree is a gentle curve in the road and a storm sewer set into the curb. All the grass and wildflowers are mashed down on one side of that third tree, and I realize this must be the tree Caroline crashed into. The grass and flowers must've been trampled during the night by EMTs and all the other responders on the scene. I can't take my eyes off that little tree.

There are already rumors about what happened, but we didn't have the details confirmed until a few days later. Mormon Trek Boulevard is a major access road to the University of Iowa and the two lanes on either side of the median are always busy. Caroline and her friend Leah Murray were coming home from a Young Life Christian meeting. They were about to part ways, Caroline on her way to the hospital to see her mom, and Leah on her way home. Caroline was riding a moped owned by some family friends that she had been riding, unbeknownst to me, for a couple of days. Leah was driving her car in the lane to the right of Caroline. As Leah pulled her car even with the moped, Caroline motioned her friend to turn up the music. Line's arm movement was enough to cause the small front tire to pull sharply left. Overcompensating, she pulled the handlebars too far to the right and the moped, traveling

35 mph, skidded out of control. Investigators concluded that Caroline was catapulted off the bike, her head struck the curb, fracturing her skull. Her body came to rest at the foot of the tree.

Pulling her car over to the side of road, Leah put on her emergency flashers and called her mom on her cell phone. "Caroline's crashed her moped and I think she broke her leg," Leah said she was horrified with the idea Line was going to miss her senior year of volleyball because she'd be on crutches.

Caroline's father Ernie told me sometime later that the medical examiner told him that Caroline's C-5 vertebra snapped and she died instantly.

Olivia Lofgren, another of Line's buddies, was traveling with her mother down Melrose in the opposite direction on the way to pick up her younger sister. Noticing Leah standing on the side of the road, Olivia yelled at her mother to pull over and she ran over to the area where a medical student and a nurse, who happened to be walking in the area when the accident occurred, were kneeling on the ground. She watched in horror as the two medical personnel worked, in vain, to resuscitate her friend.

It seems impossible that all those things – the moped, the tree, the little curve, and Line herself, helmetless, impulsive, inexperienced as a driver and moped rider – could have converged and ended her life. I keep looking at that pathetic little tree, thinking, *"One inch, one damn inch, and Line would have had a broken collar bone. She would have spent the next six weeks recuperating on the bench right next to me. Her life would have been miserable as I blamed her for our losses and for putting us in a position of not having a setter. Every time we struggled on the court I would have looked over at her and yelled, "I hope you're happy, Line. This is not what's best for West! How many times do I have to tell you?" Line would have given me her hang-dog look, and I would have forgotten I was mad at her in about two seconds.*

There's already a throng of kids standing on the median and more on the sidewalks on both sides of the street. The police stop traffic so more people who have come to mourn can safely cross. My players and Scott and I join the many others crossing Melrose Avenue. When we reach the safety of the median, the kids already standing there instinctively part, forming a tunnel for the volleyball players to pass through, and my team and I move up and encircle the tree. There's silence except for quiet weeping and the sound of cars driving slowly past as drivers gawk at the mass of people.

I've brought an old West High volleyball jersey with the number nine – the number Caroline wore – and I hang it on one of the lower branches of the third tree. I close my eyes and pray silently for a couple of minutes. My players begin to toss their flowers around the base of the small maple and other people follow suit. The ground is quickly covered with flowers, Spiderman toys—Caroline's favorite Superhero—and hundreds of rose petals. The crowd on the sidewalks bordering the accident site continues to grow. A few Iowa City High School football players, our cross-town rivals, stand alone at the edge of the crowd, silently paying their respects.

My players, Scott, and I stay at the accident site for about thirty-five minutes. I'm so focused on my own players and my own pain that I haven't paid much attention to the many faces surrounding our small group; some people have left only to be replaced by others. No one says a word. Everyone is held captive by shock and grief, lost in their own reflections.

"Ready?" I quietly ask. The girls look at me and several nod. We hold hands as we walk silently back to our cars. My soul feels empty.

# CHAPTER 10

# BACK INTO THE GYM

I get a call from Scott as I drive home from the crash site. He suggests that we hold practice tomorrow, even though we're scheduled to have this Saturday off. I agree that it's probably a good idea. The players will be better off being together, being a team, than all being separate, sitting at home alone. Scott will send every player on the team a text telling her to report to the small gym tomorrow by 8:00 am.

The next morning I'm apprehensive: I'm not sure what to expect from my players. As I walk into the small gym, the girls are sitting against the walls, putting on their practice gear. No one says a word. I look over at Scott and he shrugs, I can tell he's had the same chilly reception. Not only are our players quiet, but the stereo system hasn't been pulled out of the storage room. Caroline was always in charge of the music, and the silence only magnifies her absence. I realize I've made a huge mistake; we should have met in the team room where we watch game film that's located between the two gyms. I mistake their silence for grief, but later, when the season is over, they'll tell me over and over how furious they were in that moment, because they thought Scott and I wanted to have practice as if nothing was different. Of course, they were wrong, because my goal was for them to be together to support each other. If we were going to get through this unimaginable tragedy we'd have to do it together, as a team. We were going to have to rely on each other for support and establish bonds as strong as the bonds of any family.

I call the players to the center of the court and we sit down on the floor in a small circle. Their body language should have told me how much they resent being here: their arms are crossed and they won't look me in the eye. I wish, once again, that we were just having a meeting in the team room. Getting back on the court is just one of the many hurdles we're going to have to face this season, but it shouldn't have been today.

I slowly look around at each girl. A couple of them look up at me, but most are staring at the floor. I clear my throat. "None of us want to be in this gym today, including Scott and me. I wish I had the words to comfort you, or the wisdom to make some sense of this tragedy, but I've got nothing. I'm so angry that this has happened. It's so unfair. All I know is that Line would want us to be here together. She loved volleyball and she loved you. Volleyball is going to keep her close to us. I don't know how we're going to get through this season, but I do know we can do anything together. We're going to do everything in our power to make #9 proud. Does anyone have anything to say?" My question is met with silence. "Okay. Then let's bring it in and start practice."

Each girl slowly stands and puts a hand in the center of the huddle, all of them with their heads down and shoulders slumped.

They stand there awkwardly, right hands touching in the center of the circle. They don't know what number to count to because that was always Caroline's decision.

Shelly finally breaks the silence. "West on nine."

The girls all look at her in disbelief. Up until now they've been maintaining their composure, but their tears begin to flow as they say in unison, "One, two, three, four, five, six, seven, eight, nine; West."

Scott and I turn to each other, our eyes reflecting the grief that is coursing through our bodies. I bend over and put my hands on my knees, unsure how we can continue on with this season, as a team. The girls begin to jog around the gym, and Shelly and Kelley only make it a few steps before they collapse and lie on the floor, sobbing. Before one lap is complete, every player is crumpled on the floor. The sound of sobs and wailing fills the gym. I don't want to cry in front of the girls, but I can't stop my own tears. *This is going to be impossible,* I think. *How can anyone expect us to play volleyball without Caroline?*

Scott and I walk around the gym and try to comfort each girl. We help them to their feet and they resume their jogging, tears still streaming down their faces. Scott and I stand next to each other off the court. We don't say a word. The players finish running and slowly walk over to the ball cart. Their eyes are swollen and red, but their crying has slowed.

Volleyball players typically warm up with the same partner before every practice and match, usually one of her better friends on the team. The Russian and Squeaks are partners, Eunice and her sister Hannah always warm up together, as do Kelley and Shelly. Today when the girls start to partner up, I see Laynie hesitantly standing by the ball cart. I forgot that Line has been her warm-up partner this past week in order to help Laynie feel more included as a ninth grader. There's no one else to be her partner because without Caroline, we have an odd number of players.

"Hey, no partner warm-ups today, we're doing 9-3 Pepper," I yell loud enough to be heard above the noise of bouncing volleyballs. 9-3 Pepper is a ball-handling drill that involves a group of nine players instead of pairs. The girls quickly get the drill started. I've solved the problem with partner warm-ups for this day, but I have no idea what we're going to do for the remainder of the season.

Scott turns to me. "What are we going to do? We can't even get through warm-ups without Line."

"I haven't got a clue. There's nothing in any coaching manual to prepare you for something like this. We're going to have to coach using our gut instincts. Hopefully that'll be good enough."

He looks at me and says, "Not that it's important, but we're going to be terrible this year, aren't we?"

"Yeah, we are. We've lost our setter, our leader and identity. Our success this season will have to be measured by how well we get these kids through in one piece. I hope for their sake they can pick up a couple of wins this season, or they'll feel like they've let Caroline down."

The girls finish warming up and turn to face us; they're waiting to see what drill to do next. When I couldn't sleep the night before, I made some decisions about how to lessen the magnitude of Caroline's absence. The most important thing is for us to practice in a different environment than where we usually practice or play. Our varsity team always practices in the large gym, because it has two courts and it's where we play our matches. But we're not ready to step back in there because there would be too many reminders of Caroline. Even though the small gym only has one court, we'll continue our practices in here for the time being.

I've also decided that for now, we won't run any drills that require a setter. It would put one of our players in a very bad situation because anyone who took Caroline's place as setter would just be too uncomfortable. It's going to be difficult to have a volleyball practice without a setter, as every drill revolves around someone setting the ball. For now, Scott and I will have to be innovative.

We have the girls continue doing some easy drills. They're just going through the motions. "Scott, take over practice," I say. I step outside and stand beside the back entrance, looking out on the tennis courts. I have to do something that I've put off as long as possible.

I take out my phone from my pocket and punch the

speed dial number for the Found house.

I silently hope that the call goes straight to voicemail, but Ernie picks up on the first ring. "Hi Brez."

"Oh, Ernie," I begin to cry. "I'm so sorry."

His voice catches. "I know, Brez, I know." I can hear his sobs and they tear at my heart.

"I'm with the girls, Ernie," I eventually say. "Is there anything I can share with them as far as the visitation and funeral?"

He begins to talk, and I take notes in the margin of my practice book. "To accommodate the expected crowd, the visitation is going to be held in the West High gym on Monday. The service will be at Saint Andrew's Presbyterian Church on Tuesday. And Brez, Gregg, Catharine, and I would like you to speak at the service."

"Ernie, I would be honored." Then I ask hesitantly, "Would you like to bury Caroline in her green home jersey?"

Last night when I couldn't sleep, I thought about how important volleyball was to Line. Even though she played basketball and softball, volleyball was her passion. It seems appropriate that she should be buried in the uniform that she dreamed of wearing ever since her big sister Catharine played four years earlier. I should have asked my athletic director if I could make this offer, but I didn't care if I got in trouble for it. I wanted her in her uniform.

"Caroline has been cremated and her organs and tissues were donated. It'd be wonderful though, if we could put her jersey on the closed casket."

"Absolutely, Ernie, anything you want. I'll be in touch." Before I end the call I say, "I love you."

"I love you too," he replies.

I put my phone away. *Why did I just tell Ernie that I loved him? I've only talked to the man a couple times during Catharine and Caroline's volleyball career, and we don't have that close of a relationship. I hope he didn't feel that I was being inappropriate for saying that to him.*

On another day, in a different time, I would maybe be embarrassed for saying those three words to him, but now they just feel natural.

I go back into the gym and call the girls over. They listen intently as I share Ernie's information. If they're surprised that the visitation will be at West High, they don't show it. My players trudge out of the gym in small groups and head to their cars. The girls are getting together in the afternoon to put together a collage of their favorite pictures of Caroline to display at the visitation. I'm relieved that they'll be together for the remainder of the day. Scott and I walk out to the parking lot and when I reach my vehicle, I give him a hug.

"Thanks, Scott," I say as I open my car door. "I don't know what I'd do without you."

When I get home I lean down and hug Charlie, grab a Miller Chill lime beer from the refrigerator and head outside. I sit in the gazebo and crack open the beer. Hell, it's only ten in the morning, but at this point I want the numbing effects of alcohol, anything to dull the pain. Charlie, sensing my mood, is subdued. I slump over on the love seat and he jumps up and snuggles next to me, leaning his head on my shoulder. I put my arm around him and shut my eyes. I want to rewind the clock twenty-four hours and have the chance to look at Caroline's senior pictures. I want the chance to ask her about the moped. I want the chance to do everything over.

I've begun to doze off when the sound of the phone interrupts my rest. It's my good friend Tom Keating. Tom is one of the greatest volleyball coaches in the nation. When he was the coach at Wahlert High School in Dubuque, his teams won eleven state titles. He's currently the principal at Cedar Rapids Xavier High School and no longer a varsity coach due to the time demands of being an administrator. He's the person I've always turned to when I needed some coaching advice, and now he inherently knew I needed him for some life advice. Tom knew Caroline, and if anyone will understand what our team's going through, he will.

He listens patiently while I vent my anger at God. When I'm finished, he quietly reassures me that God has things taken care of. Then he says, "Brez, your first inclination and that of your players will be to cancel the season, or simply do whatever's necessary to get by." I *was* ready to write off the season, not literally cancel the season, but just do whatever to get through the season as quickly as possible

"Don't do that!" he said. "It would be unfair to you, your kids, West High, and most of all to Caroline. Get through the heartache of the next few days and then you need to get that team on track. Get them back to doing what they do best: volleyball. Volleyball is what's going to get all of you through. If anyone is capable of leading a team through this tragedy, it's you. Do what you do best: coach!

"And," he continues, "be very careful that your players don't say they want to win for Caroline. That'll become a lose/lose situation. Every time they drop a match, they'll feel like they've let her down. Instead, encourage them to play like Caroline—that'll change their entire focus. Lastly, don't be afraid to ask your friends for help. People will be there for you, Brez, including me."

We talk a bit more and I thank him one more time, before setting the phone down. I know his words will help me get through the dark days ahead. I put my head in my hands and begin to weep. I don't know when I'll ever be done crying.

## CHAPTER 11

# THE VISITATION

It's early Monday morning and once again, we're holding practice in the back gym. We're not here to improve our volleyball skills, I just want my girls to get together as much as possible so they can support each other. This ten a.m. practice will get us out of the gym before the funeral directors from the funeral home begin preparations for the visitation. The players struggle like they did on Saturday. Even the simplest volleyball skills have become difficult.

We're an hour into practice when I hear a noise in the lobby between the two gyms. Twenty feet away from our gym entrance, a hearse is backing up to the double doorway, directed by a man in a black suit. The vehicle stops, another man gets out, and the two men open the back door of the hearse and gently roll a casket out onto a gurney. I watch in horror as they push the casket into the main gym. I didn't want the girls here during the preparations for Caroline's visitation. Ernie didn't say what the visitation would involve, but I know Caroline's not in that casket, because Ernie said she was cremated after her organs were harvested. But the girls won't know that, and the sight of this coffin will be more than they can bear.

My mind reels; I'm not sure what we should do now. There's no escaping the fact that the girls are going to see all the activity going on. I beckon Scott over and tell him that we misjudged how early they would start to set things up. We agree that our only option is for the two of us to take all the girls into the other gym, where they're setting up the visitation. We need to do this now, as soon as we're done with practice. We all need to walk in that gym together.

We finish up with practice and the girls begin to do their cool down stretching. From their quick glances into the large gym, I can tell that they realize what's happening in there. I join their circle and say, "I want to apologize. I thought we'd be done before any of this started but I was wrong. How about we go in there together?"

Several of the girls nod their heads and we walk over to the main gym entrance. I take a deep breath and enter the area that has always felt like home, with the girls following closely behind. They all join hands before stepping over the threshold. The gym already looks different. Flower arrangements and potted plants are set up along the walls and across the middle of the floor. The fragrance is overwhelming and to me, nauseating: our gym smells like a funeral home.

We move around the perimeter and the girls stop and look somberly at the posters filled with pictures of Caroline and her friends. The softball, basketball, and volleyball teams with whom she played have all put together collages, and so have many of Line's other friends.

We all avoid looking at the coffin sitting in the center of the gym. It's almost like we've made a silent pact – if we don't look at Caroline's coffin and acknowledge its existence, then maybe none of this is really happening. This gym used to represent the joy and fun of our athletic endeavors. I wonder if my players will ever feel that way again. After twenty minutes of walking around, we say our goodbyes and agree to meet back at school an hour before the visitation is scheduled to begin.

We're all in the team room by five that evening. I know the girls need to compose themselves before they go through this heart-wrenching experience. They're wearing their uniform tops and Scott, Ashten, our sophomore coach, and I are dressed as we would for a game: khaki shorts and West High polo shirts.

We walk out to meet Line's family: father Ernie, sister Catharine, and brother Gregg, and their extensive extended family of aunts, uncles, grandparents and cousins. Ellyn is too sick to attend her daughter's visitation. My heart sinks, I feel so badly for Ernie. I can't fathom how heartbroken he must be right now.

Ernie meets us before we're even halfway across the gym floor and he collectively draws the team into his arms and consoles each player. I offer what I think are probably lame condolences to Ernie and Line's other family members, but it's impossible for me to pull my eyes away from the casket, sitting like an island in the center of the court. It's bitterly ironic to me that the funeral directors put this casket on the setter's spot, the very place where Caroline stood and orchestrated so many triumphs.

The team and I walk over to the casket. Line's senior picture sits atop the closed lid and her number nine home jersey is draped over the side. I'm astonished by how pretty and mature Caroline looks in her senior portrait. How did I not notice that she had changed from a young teen into an adult, her youthful face transformed into the face of a beautiful young woman? Her blond hair falls over the shoulders of her simple white dress and her face wears just a hint of that famous Caroline smile. At this moment it hits me—she's truly gone. I vowed that I was going to be strong for the girls, but I can't stop my tears. I make no attempt to wipe them away as they drip down onto my shirt.

People begin to arrive much earlier than the five o'clock starting time. The line begins to snake out both main entrances of the gymnasium. The queue goes up one side of the gym floor, around the endline and then back across the center of the gym past the casket. Thousands of people have come to pay their respects, and many will have to wait over two hours to even get through the gym doors. Ernie, the consummate gentleman, stands ten feet away from his daughter's casket and hugs each and every person. He awes me with his strength and composure. Often Catharine and Gregg join him, but for the majority of the time he stands alone.

Scott, the girls, and I stay together on one end of the gymnasium. It's as if we're afraid to separate because of the strength we draw from each other. I glance at the gym entrance and I see the entire Cedar Rapids Washington volleyball team and their coach, Kari Lombardi, come in. The girls are wearing their varsity uniform tops to demonstrate their support of our team. I wonder whether I would have pulled my team out of preseason practice if the roles were reversed. I'd like to think so, but at the same time I have hard time imagining cancelling practice to go to a visitation for someone none of us knew and only played against once or twice. Once again, I'm astonished by how many people – people who didn't know Caroline at all – are here. My players, Scott, and I walk over to greet the Washington team, and Kari pulls me into a strong embrace.

"Brez, we're so sorry," she says quietly. "Caroline was truly a joy to watch on the court."

I'm numb. I can only nod and thank them for coming. Their kindness overwhelms me. Before the night is over, this scene will be repeated over and over as almost every school in our conference walks in and pays their respects. Iowa City High arrives soon after Cedar Rapids Washington. Rivalries with City High aside, Coach Craig Pitcher and his girls come early. When they first arrive, Erin Muir, City High's setter, walks over to me. She had played club ball with Line and they'd become good friends. We hug and she begins crying, sobs wracking her body, and once again I realize how many people loved Caroline.

It's a human tendency to eulogize people when they die, but Caroline really was one of those unique individuals who had an impact on everyone she met. Her antics and deep laughter were infectious, but there was more to her than just being goofy. Twice I mentioned to her that one of my ninth-grade students was eating alone in my classroom because they were autistic or had some other problem. She promptly showed up in my classroom—where the student would be isolating themselves from the social gatherings of the lunch room—extended her hand and said, "Hi, I'm Caroline. I'd love to be your friend." The struggling student's face lit up and the two of them began talking away, sitting close together on the sofa, next to the back wall of my room. I was always so proud of her during those moments. That was the true Caroline. She loved people as much as she loved life.

That's why her death seems so senseless and has affected so many people. Not just the coaches and players on our team and the Found family, but all the students and staff at West, much of the Iowa City community, and many people throughout the state. Her death is a stark reminder that there aren't any guarantees in life, and that we need to be passionate in our pursuit of happiness. Line wasn't a gifted athlete, but she worked hard to become a great setter. She wasn't a scholar, but she worked diligently to be on the honor roll. She put everything she had into everything she did. That's how Line lived every day of her short life.

The night drags on and I look at my watch. It's only been three hours, but it feels like three days. I step away from the group and gingerly make my way up the bleachers. I need to be alone. I sit and bury my head in my arms, oblivious of my surroundings. I'm not alone for long. I feel someone take both my hands in theirs, look up and see Olivia Mekies, Squeaks, standing in front of me. I can see the concern and empathy reflected in her eyes.

"Just take a deep breath," she says. "We can do this together."

This is the first time I've seen Squeaks step into a nurturing role. Squeaks seems to have an innate ability to sense when someone needs comforting.

She sits down next to me and I put my arm around her shoulder. Three years ago, Squeaks' older sister, Erika, was my assistant coach. I was concerned then about what would happen when Squeaks was old enough to play varsity volleyball for West. I didn't think she was going to be mentally tough enough to be a starter for our team. Having her on the bench, not playing, while her sister was my assistant coach, could have been a potentially awkward situation. Now I don't know what I would do without her. We lean our heads together and watch the unending line of people waiting to offer their condolences to Ernie.

"Squeaks, thank you," I tell her and she squeezes my hand in response. I'm going to have to rely on my girls this season for comfort and support. I've always felt there should be a barrier between coaches and their players, that there shouldn't be relationships off the court. But that long-standing philosophy has been shattered.

## CHAPTER 12

# GOODBYE FRIEND

St. Andrew's parking lot is not going to be large enough to accommodate the expected crowd for Caroline's funeral Mass, so our team agrees to park at Finkbine golf course, about a half mile from the church, leaving the six parking spots we'd take up at the church open for other people. No one says a word as we gather together in a circle in the golf course parking lot. With clenched jaws and somber faces, the girls seemed determined to maintain their composure. When our last player arrives, we begin our slow walk to the church, each person tightly holding the hand of the person next to her.

We step into the church lobby and immediately Dan Ciha, the funeral director, comes up to greet us. "Follow me, girls. We have a private room for you to be together until the services begin."

We follow him down the hallway and he opens a door and indicates with an outstretched hand that this room is where we should wait. There are nineteen of us and we barely fit into the small area. A few players sit, but most of us simply lean against the walls; no one says a word. I watch the second hand of the clock make its designated rounds. It feels like we're on death row.

I keep an eye on my players to make sure they're holding up. They all look resolutely composed, as if crying would be a sign of weakness or even a betrayal of Caroline. When we walked in, everybody else in the foyer was crying, but my girls seem determined not to. We all jump when a tap on the door breaks the silence. Dan sticks his head in and silently beckons us to follow him. We walk through the packed foyer and people turn to watch us pass. A few of them catch my eye and nod sympathetically as we walk up the aisle between the rows of pews to the front of the church. The three rows nearest the casket and podium have been reserved for the volleyball team, but I saw a few of her softball and basketball teammates scattered throughout the church. I step into the first row of seats, followed by Kelley, Shelly and Squeaks.

The church is overflowing. I look around at all the people and recognize hundreds of West High students. My heart aches for every one of them. Most of them look like they've been crying for hours, even days. The three rows on our left remain conspicuously empty. Those seats will soon be filled with members of the Found family. After the service is over, I'll learn that there were so many people here, some had to be directed to small rooms reserved for crying infants, while others watched the service on closed-circuit television out in the church lobby.

One of Caroline's cousins walks to the front and begins to sing a hauntingly beautiful song to signal the start of the services. The crowd turns as one to watch the pall bearers grimly push the casket up the center aisle with the family coming after: Gregg and Catharine walk side by side, Ernie pushes Ellyn in a wheelchair, and the rest of Caroline's extended family follows.

I've overheard that many people thought that Ellyn would be too sick to attend the services, and even Ernie didn't know whether she'd be able to come. I'm not surprised to see her—I didn't think anything would keep her away—but I'm shocked, not by the fact that she's here, but by her appearance. I haven't seen her since she attended a softball game Caroline was playing in a month earlier. She looked fine then. Now her once-beautiful face is drawn and gaunt, her body ravaged by her deadly opponent. I watch Ernie help her out of her wheelchair and onto the pew, and then I avert my eyes. It's simply too difficult to see this proud and private family with their grief on public display.

Several people eulogize Caroline and reminisce about her antics, her love of dancing, her connection with people and her passion for life. Finally it's my turn to talk about the girl we all loved. I walk up to the podium, take a big breath, and begin. I talk about the qualities that made Caroline unique, from the perspective of her coach and teacher: her spontaneity and inclusiveness, her sense of humor. People in the church laugh when I describe how she used to wipe her forehead on the coaches' sleeves during matches and the way she always made goofy faces in front of a camera. I share the story about when I told her I was going to have a bracelet made with the initials WIBFW (What Is Best For West) to remind her to curb her enthusiasm until more appropriate moments.

Taking a deep breath, I continue:

"Thinking about it now…What is Best For West? Caroline Found was what was best for West. To her friends, please embody those characteristics that set Line apart…her sense of humor, her zest for life, and her compassion for others. That will be her legacy. We will never order another #9 jersey…no one else could fill those shoes. Caroline, I promise we will do you proud this season."

As I make my way back to my seat, I can see my girls trying to stifle smiles behind their hands. Before I can sit down Kelley whispers to me to turn around; I do and I can feel her tugging at something on my butt. I glance back and realize I had a tissue stuck to my pants the entire time I was talking. I am mortified, and hope that only my players could see it. I can't help but think that Line – the spirit of Line, the invisible, no-longer-physically-present Line who still somehow seems to be among us – has something to do with this embarrassing moment. If she could have found a way to do something during this funeral, that is what she would have done.

As the service continues, I can't keep myself from sneaking glances at the Founds. I'm struck by the complete and unadulterated love I see in Ellyn's eyes every time she looks up at Ernie. Ernie would tower over her even if she were standing but she's not. She's seated in the pew, where even through her pain and illness and under the influence of what must be a lot of medication, she keeps making eye contact with Ernie. Every time she looks at him, Ernie leans down and squeezes her shoulder, and I see the same love in his eyes I see in hers. It's as if they're drawing strength from each other, and they know their opportunities to do that are numbered.

The funeral ends and the family members rise to exit the church. We watch as Ernie prepares to help Ellyn back into the wheelchair. With a shake of her head, she refuses the aid of the chair, and grasping her husband's arm, she begins to slowly walk up the aisle. She reaches out and takes someone's hand at the end of every pew, finding the strength – this proud and determined woman – to take her final steps as a tribute to her daughter. There is not a dry eye in the church.

I spend the next hour and a half talking, consoling and at times being consoled by the hundreds of people who remain at the church after the services. Some people are eating sandwiches and cookies provided by the church community while others, particularly the high school students, are standing quietly in small groups. At times there is laughter as someone tells a favorite story about Caroline—usually about some shenanigan or prank that she pulled—but mostly there is a profound sense of disbelief that Line is gone.

Now all I want to do is escape all this emotion and return to the solitude of my home. I want to sit next to Charlie in the gazebo and take off these dang heels. But different people stop me as I make my way through the remaining mourners, and it's another thirty minutes before I reach my car. The trapped August heat rolls over me as I open the door. It's too warm to get in the car so I pull my cell phone from the glove compartment. I have two missed calls and three texts.

The voice mails and texts are all from Ernie and I can tell he first tried to contact me right after the funeral was over. I hit play and his tired voice fills my ear. "Brez, it's Ernie. We're taking Ellyn out to the farm for an hour or so and we'd like you to join us. I know she'd love to have a chance to talk to you."

I read his texts and his last one confirms what I already imagined:  it was written two hours after the end of the funeral, and he said they were taking Ellyn back to the hospital. Just like I missed the opportunity to look at Caroline's senior pictures, I've missed my opportunity to talk to Ellyn one last time.

## CHAPTER 13
# LIFE WITHOUT LINE

The day after the funeral, a Wednesday, we gather in the back gym to officially begin our life without Caroline. The players are listless and want to be anywhere else but here. I feel lethargic as well.

We sit along the gym wall and watch the dance squad as they finish up with their scheduled practice time. I see the tears begin to roll down Kelley's face as she sits next to me. I need to somehow lighten the mood of my players. "Come on everybody let's go show the dance team how it's done!" I yell running out to the middle of the floor.

My fifteen girls look at me as if I'm crazy. I grab an extra set of pom poms that are sitting on the floor, and yell to the dance coach, "Crank up the music, I'm ready to roll!"

The dance squad members smile at my flailing arms and uncoordinated steps. I have no idea what I'm doing and I certainly couldn't keep up with their dancing. I almost fall down when I try to imitate one of their jump turns. Stopping to catch my breath, I yell at my players to join in. After some coaxing, they slowly stand up and make another row in back of the dancers. We unsuccessfully try to follow the dancers' choreographed competition routine. Soon every girl on my team is laughing so hard they've got tears in their eyes, but this time they're tears of laughter. The dance squad members seem to be having as much fun as we are. The song ends and I thank their coach for allowing us to interrupt their practice. *Jumping into the dance routine is the type of stunt that Line might have done, and I'm sure I would have scolded her,* I think. I'm not sure if I was trying to imitate her or whether I was just being goofy, but humor and outrageous behavior might be our saving grace this season.

We set up the nets and I turn my attention back to the problem at hand, which is that we do not have a setter. Scott and I have to figure out who can run the offense this season. We will try different varsity kids in Caroline's position: Kelley Fliehler, Olivia Fairfield, Erin Weathers and Laynie Whitehead, but at this moment, I can't see anyone filling Line's position. It'll be a daunting task to find a setter, not only because of the skill requirements, but the pressure of taking Caroline's spot. We have to put one of our girls in a very difficult position. Like it or not, I know that one of these young women will have to assume that responsibility.

The gym seems so quiet without Line's music, laughter and energy. I call the girls over after an unproductive two hours. They form a semi-circle around Scott and I in the center of the court.

Following Tom's advice, I begin. "Listen. I think we need to establish some guidelines for this season. We absolutely can't dedicate this season to Caroline. Please don't compete with the thought that we have to win for her. That'll be an impossible burden for you. Instead, our goal should be to play like Line. Every time we step onto the court, we should try to emulate her joy of playing volleyball and her unbridled enthusiasm. Let's remember all her best qualities and bring them with us to every practice and match." The girls sit quietly, processing what I've just said.

Hannah Infelt breaks the silence. "I have something else to add. We can never cry on the court. Line would hate that! If you know you're going to cry, then step out of practice and do what you need to do, but it can't happen between the lines."

The girls nod their heads in assent. Hannah is a strong and opinionated young woman, but she's usually quiet during volleyball practice. In the past she's always taken a backseat to the boisterous posturing of Line and Shelly—a laughing bystander, but not a participant. This is a breakthrough for her to speak up in practice, and I'm proud of her. I understand her rationale and I think it's a positive suggestion. Perhaps she'll assume the leadership of the team that we lost when we lost Caroline.

Olivia Fairfield tells everyone that her mom is ordering purple "Live Like Line" bracelets for the team, and other people can purchase one for two dollars. "Also," she continues, "I think we should all get the Live Like Line shirts to wear on game days."

Over the weekend, two of Caroline's friends, Maddie Vernon and Kaitlyn Robinson coined the phrase 'Live Like Line' as a way to honor her. The shirts were as bright as Caroline's personality – bright blue with pumpkin orange outlining the white lettering. The word spread very quickly through social media, and Maddie's father, Mark, the owner of Hollywood Graphics, was shocked by the hundreds of orders that had already been placed. Before the week ended, over 1500 t-shirts had been ordered.

No one else has anything more to add, so Shelly puts her hand in the center of the circle and the other girls follow her example as she yells, "West on nine!" Caroline's number.

Everyone huddles up, and we again count from one through nine to end practice. That cheer will be the way we end every one of our huddles for the rest of the season.

## CHAPTER 14

# LIVE LIKE LINE: EMPATHY

It's four days after Caroline's funeral, and we're hosting a twelve-team scrimmage. The other teams have been quickly averting their eyes when they walk in and see the West High players. It feels like we have leprosy, but I understand. They're teenagers and don't know how to approach my players after our loss. There's no protocol. My players are also to blame. I can see by their tightly clenched jaws that they've put up protective barriers that scream: Leave us alone!

All the teams start to warm up and Roxanne Paulsen, the varsity coach at Marion High School, comes over. She gives me a warm embrace and says, "Kathy, we're so sorry about Caroline." She hands me a plastic baggy filled with green bracelets. "We had enough of these made for your team. There are a few extra to pass out to anyone else that you want. Hopefully they'll always be a reminder to you and your players that you're in our hearts and prayers."

I open the zip-lock baggy and remove one of the bracelets. One side of the plastic band reads 'Live Like Line' in contrasting white, surrounded by two volleyballs and a simple crucifix.

"Oh, Roxanne, thank you so much. I can't even begin to tell you how much this means to all of us."

We hug one more time and I walk away. I'm awed by everyone's generosity and thoughtfulness. I look around the gym and begin to notice that many teams are wearing hair ribbons decorated with LLL or #9. I think about the hundreds of coaches, players, and volleyball officials who have expressed their condolences, support, and love this past week.

We scrimmage five teams. Our play on the court is sporadic as different players step into the setting position. Each time we try a new person as the setter, we have to move other players to different positions to accommodate the change. To be successful in volleyball, it's imperative to have continuity with your starting rotations. It's one of the more difficult team sports to be successful at, because every contact of the ball is dependent on another person. Players have to be comfortable with the person next to them on the court. When a volleyball team is playing well, it's a moment of beauty. No other sport resembles the cooperative effort of volleyball.

We do not have this chemistry today. I feel like we're in a small shanty fighting a tsunami without any paddles. My players aren't communicating with each other and balls are dropping to the floor. The hitters are struggling because the sets are so poor. We'll be lucky to finish with a .500 season.

We huddle up. "Not a bad job today, girls. We're on the right track," I tell them. They look at me like I'm crazy. I mentally hit myself on the head: *Don't try to con these young women. They're volleyball savvy and I need to be truthful.*

"Okay, so maybe it wasn't the best volleyball we've ever played, but hang in there, we'll get better," I say. "Don't forget the photo shoot for the poster tomorrow. Seniors, please stay for a second after everyone leaves."

The seven seniors join Scott and me, and we all sit on the floor toward the back of the gym near the open door. I know they're tired and want to go home.

"Tell me about what we're going to put on the poster. What's the plan?" I ask.

All the West High athletic teams pose for a team

poster prior to the season. Generally there's a catch phrase or play on words that's the motto for that season. We usually have 250 posters printed, which are given out free of charge to anyone who wants one. Teachers display them on their classroom doors or in their rooms. Students tape them in their lockers and businesses that donate money to defray the cost of production prominently display them in their windows.

I never get involved with the team poster. The girls come up with the theme and I provide feedback on its appropriateness. Caroline was excited when she came to me during the preseason this year and said the poster was going to boldly feature the 2010 state championship trophy. The words, "REMEMBER US?" were going to be written boastfully across the bottom. It would've been brazen and cocky, but I gave my approval. *If they had the confidence to back up that statement,* I thought, *it's fine with me.* But now things have changed for us.

The girls look around at each other and finally Shelly looks at me defiantly—as if challenging me to veto their idea—and says, "We're going to have 'Remember us...' with Caroline photo-shopped into the group picture."

My heart lurches. The poster that was going to be the epitome of brashness will now become a memorial. The girls and Scott watch for my reaction. "Nice job, you guys," my voice catches. "I'm sure it will be wonderfully done. Thanks. Head on home and get some rest."

The senior girls stand wearily and head toward the back door of the gym without saying a word. Their shirts are soaked with sweat from playing volleyball for the past three hours. I remain seated, pretending to be looking at some notes. Scott looks at me inquiringly, his blue eyes searching mine for what I want him to do. He's such a sensitive guy that I know he doesn't want to leave me sitting there alone.

"Do you want to talk about how we played today or anything?" he asks.

"Naw, it's all good. You go ahead, I'm just going to

write down some things before I forget." My voice catches, and I think he intuitively knows that I'm on the verge of tears.

Scott leans down. "Don't forget, I'm here if you need me." He gives me a hug before following the same path the girls took moments before.

I didn't ask who came up with the poster idea, and it doesn't really matter. I never considered the possibility that our photographer, Mike Jenn, would be able to put Line on the poster. Even though she's not with us physically, every one of us can feel her presence—especially on the volleyball court—so it makes sense to have her image on our team poster.

I put my head down on my bended knees, cross my arms in front of me, and sob. I miss Caroline so much. At this moment, all I can think about is how incredibly difficult even the simplest of tasks have become.

Before the season is over, we'll have to reorder three more printings of the poster, with the picture above the two unassuming words, "Remember us."

# CHAPTER 15

# ELLYN

It's 8:00 on Tuesday evening, one week after Caroline's funeral, and I'm reading the newspaper and relaxing in my gazebo. As always, Charlie's by my side. Last year he was picked up as a stray in Anamosa, Iowa, and no one claimed him. When I saw his picture on a pet rescue website, I was haunted by his caramel brown eyes pleading to be rescued. He was only three days from being euthanized, and I knew I needed to make the forty-five-minute drive to the Anamosa vet clinic and at least meet him. When they brought him out of his kennel, he ran over to where I was sitting, wedged himself between my knees and tilted his head back to look up at me. He had several gaping wounds on his head and his long brownish-red hair was matted with what smelled like cow manure, but none of that mattered—one look into his eyes and I was smitten. I completed the required paperwork and took him home with me. He's been my constant companion ever since, never leaving my side when I'm home.

My phone begins to ring and I try to ignore the insistent sound. I don't want to talk to anyone. Finally I glance at the screen ID and see that it's Hannah Infelt calling, and pick up. I hear sobbing on the other end of the line. *Oh no, what now?*

"Brez," Hannah says, "Ellyn died." Hannah starts crying again. "How much more can we take?" she chokes out between sobs.

My heart sinks at the news. I wonder the same thing.

These girls haven't even begun to recover from Caroline's death, and now they'll be going to another visitation and funeral. They're just kids, but they've already lost their innocence.

My attempts to comfort Hannah are futile. She's inconsolable. We end our conversation and then I call Scott and tell him the sad news.

"Scott. Hannah just called to tell me that Ellyn died."

There is silence and finally he replies, "I feel so horrible for Ernie, Catharine, and Gregg. This wasn't how things were meant to be, it's just not right."

"I agree. This is worse than any nightmare. It all seems surreal. I'll text all the girls in case some of them haven't heard. This is going to be a huge emotional setback. You and I have to be prepared to do whatever we can to help them at practice tomorrow."

We say our good-byes. I'm angry and overwhelmed by emotion. I want to scream at the heavens. I want to hit something. I want to rewind our lives and have a do-over. I throw the newspaper on the ground and pace back and forth on my patio.

Poor Ellyn, I think. It's only been four months since her diagnosis. She was the picture of health right up until her diagnosis in April, and she even looked fine for a while after that. When I saw her at Caroline's West High softball games during the summer, she looked totally normal. At that time it was impossible to believe she was failing in her fight with pancreatic cancer.

I think of how Ernie and Ellyn looked at each other during the funeral. I remember how the two of them went to New Hampshire every August to climb Mount Monadnock and renew their wedding vows. The two of them planned this annual trek at the end of the softball season and before volleyball preseason practices started so that Caroline, and before her, Catharine, could get back in time to join our team. Caroline would always come back and tell us stories about how the climb went. This year when Ellyn was too ill to climb the mountain, her three children made the three-hour trek up the mountain on her behalf. Caroline posted many pictures on Facebook of herself standing proudly on the mountaintop with Catharine and Gregg, the three of them wearing their purple "Team Ellyn" shirts. This was less than two weeks before Line had her moped accident.

Ernie adored his wife. For his and Ellyn's twenty-fifth wedding anniversary, he commissioned a local artist to reproduce Grant Wood's American Gothic portrait, with twenty-five items representing each of his and Ellyn's years together hidden in the painting. He hung the resulting artwork prominently above the fireplace in their living room, and took great delight in explaining the symbolic meaning of each hidden gem to anyone who visited.

I stop walking and sit back down. How will the Found family find the strength to go on? At the very least, this unfathomable tragedy will change Ernie. A skilled pianist, master story-teller, and expert magician, Ernie loves to make people laugh. It's easy to see where his younger daughter got her personality. Now he's lost both his soul-mate and his baby in a span of ten days—I can't imagine how he'll ever come to terms with the magnitude of the loss. Gregg and Catharine have lost both their sister and their mother, and that has to be equally devastating for them. But Ernie's going to have to walk into his empty house, haunted by the memories of his marriage and earlier family life, every night. *Sometimes life is so unfair,* I think.

Ellyn was a second mother to the seniors on the team, and she had all the girls out for pool parties, sleepovers, and barn dances. They all loved her. I believe a few of them have been holding onto hope that her health would take a miraculous turn. They're all so fragile, and I wish I could magically erase their pain. I know they didn't envision their senior year in high school being consumed by grief and mourning.

The next morning I'm sitting in my locker room office during my third hour prep, or non-teaching, period. Lost in my thoughts, I don't hear Kelley and Squeaks walk in.

"Can we talk to you?" Kelley says.

Startled from my reverie, I can only nod. It's immediately apparent from their red and swollen eyes that the two of them have been crying. Without anyone saying a word, I take Squeak's and Kelley's arms and lead them out to the hallway.

"Don't you two have class this period?" I ask.

"I was in Mr. Lindsey's American Humanities and I got a text from Kelley to meet her in the bathroom near the main office," Squeaks says.

"Did Mr. Lindsey give you permission to leave class?" I ask her.

"No, I just got up and left."

"Kelley, what about you?"

She hesitates for a second. "I just got up and left as well. Our teachers understand."

This isn't the first time one of my girls has left during a class. Sometimes they've told their teachers that they need to come see me, and I know there have been other times that they've left to talk to Amy Kanellis, our guidance counselor, or simply found a friend or teammate.

Hannah Infelt and Emily Nicholson, another of Caroline's friends, are walking towards us and join us near the gym doors. I can see that all four girls are overcome by emotion. I don't want others witnessing this private moment, and redirect them outside to a bench in front of the school.

Their tears begin to flow. Their eyes reflect their pain and I choke up with emotion. What else can I say to them that I haven't already said over and over for the past ten days?

I look at Emily and it occurs to me that she probably has more wisdom than I have when it comes to personal loss.

I was introduced to the Nicholson family a few years back when Tonya, Emily's older sister, participated in our Top Dog volleyball program. Over time, I learned that they were avid Green Bay Packer fans like I am. Tragically, Tonya died during her sophomore year at West—Emily was only a seventh grader then. Emily's parents, Dave and Amy, have been very solicitous during Line's visitation and the few times they've been at school. They've been a source of hope and encouragement to me and my team. Last week, Amy gave me the book "*Heaven is For Real*" by Todd Burpol, saying she felt I might be comforted by it.

"Em, I know Caroline's and Ellyn's deaths have probably triggered many memories for you. I hope you don't mind me asking, but how did you and your family manage to cope during those dark days?"

Emily pushes a few strands of strawberry-blonde hair away from her face, squeezes Kelley's hand, and takes a deep breath. "I cried, I prayed, and I tried to focus on breathing when things seemed darkest. You guys, you have to ask for help when you need it, and take things slowly. You won't feel better for a long time. Don't forget that we're all in this together, and you're not alone."

I give Emily a hug and the four of us sit outside for another thirty minutes, until the next class period. We don't talk much, but the girls seem to draw comfort by taking a time-out from their school day. It's hard to go through the motions of normalcy when your heart tells you that nothing will ever be normal again.

Three days later the team meets at St. Andrew's for Ellyn's visitation, the same church where Ellyn resolutely walked up the aisle at the end of her daughter's funeral ten days ago. The girls, Scott, and I wait in line to meet Ernie. When it's my turn, I hug him and say how sorry I am and he looks at me. "Brez, my life has been blessed," he says.

I think about his words as I hug Gregg and Catharine. His life has been blessed? How can he possibly say that?

His world was torn upside down four months ago with the words "Stage 4 pancreatic cancer." All the things he and Ellyn would have experienced—watching Caroline play her senior year of volleyball, grandchildren, retirement in New Hampshire—swept away in the blink of an eye. If it had been me, I might have been able to come to terms with the cancer, but there's no way I could have ever accepted the cruel twist of fate with Line's death. I would be angry at the world. Not so Ernie. Those simple words will forever change how I look at him. What a remarkable man.

I continue through the receiving line, offering my condolences to the same family members I offered them to ten days ago at Caroline's visitation. All of Ellyn's sisters—she had six—seem to have aged even more since I saw them two weeks ago.

When I get to the end of the receiving line, I turn and wait for my players. Gradually, one by one, they come and stand by my side. I watch Kelley and Shelly hug Catharine and turn away. The two of them furtively swipe at their tears as they make their way to our small group. I give each of them a reassuring hug and we all walk out to the darkness together.

## CHAPTER 16

# THE SEASON BEGINS

Last night, the night before Ellyn's visitation, we officially started the 2011 season. We played against Bettendorf for the first game of the MVC/MAC Challenge, a round-robin weeknight tournament between three schools in our conference—the Mississippi Valley—and three teams from the Mississippi Athletic Conference.

I could tell my players were dreading the match. They looked weary, sad, and unsure of themselves, and walked into the gym slowly. Sweat was soaking through their shirts, and I couldn't tell if it was because of the humidity or their nervousness, or both. Several well-intentioned people came up to us on our way into the gym to offer their condolences, but with each hug the girls looked more forlorn.

I sat on the team bench. My players began to put on their knee pads and switch to their court shoes. I reached into my briefcase and pulled out Caroline's musty shoes that she had written on to honor her mom. I teared up and looked at Scott.

"We agreed, under the first chair, right?" I asked him.

He nodded and I set Line's shoes under the first chair of our team bench. I had gone back and forth in my mind about the appropriateness of having her shoes displayed, but I wanted part of her near us during matches. When I discussed it with Scott, we agreed that if they were under the bench, they wouldn't really be "on display" to the public—I wanted them there just for us—

not anyone else. It was a no-brainer to have them under the first chair, that's where I always had her sit if I pulled her from a match to talk to her.

Scott put his arm around my shoulder. I shut my eyes tightly, to try to hold my emotions in check. I thought about how much Caroline loved competition. She would have been ecstatic to be starting her senior volleyball season. If she had been here, she would have been jumping up and down and screaming and yelling at her teammates, whipping them up to her level of excitement. The players would have been more interested in Line's antics than in warming up for the match. I probably would have already admonished her, saying something like, 'Caroline! If you don't mind, please stop screwing around and warm up before the match begins!"

Someone tapped me on the shoulder. "Sorry to bother you, Coach. If you don't mind, we'd like to interview you and a couple of your players?"

I turned around. Standing behind our bench were camera crews and reporters from three different television stations. This was something I hadn't anticipated, but probably should have. My natural inclination was to shelter my kids as much as possible, and I didn't want our raw grief broadcast on television. I told the reporters that I would talk to them, but the girls were off limits. I answered a few questions about who was going to set for us now and about my expectations for the season.

Finally one reporter asked me, "How's the team doing?"

I wanted to scream, "How the heck do you think they're doing? Their leader, captain, and best friend is dead at the age of seventeen! What kind of asinine question is that?' Instead, I said politely that they were doing as well as could be expected under the circumstances, and then I excused myself from any more questions.

Two officials came up to me. "Coach, we need your

captain for the coin toss."

*Oh my God,* I thought. *I've been coaching for twenty-two years and I didn't even remember we needed to have a captain for a coin toss.* I hadn't even thought to designate someone to Caroline's place. My mind went blank.

"Kelley, Shelly, Olivia, Squeaks, Hannah and Anna," I finally barked, "go be captains." No team ever has more than two or three captains but I didn't care, I thought, *mine is going to have six.* The seven of us joined the two officials and Diane Lichtenburg, the Bettendorf coach, and her captains. The official flipped the coin and we were designated the home team and Bettendorf, the visiting team, would be serving first.

Finally it was time to step onto the court. Our hitters took turns warming up, hitting off sets from Kelley and Eunice. The idea was to use them both as setters tonight. It was far from an ideal situation since Eunice was a middle hitter and Kelley played back court. But with only a few days to prepare for this match, Scott and I hadn't come up with any better options.

Then, with only three minutes remaining until the start of the match, the girls started poking each other and whispering to each other. I turned around and looked in the direction they were all looking in. I saw Caroline's family, Ernie, Gregg, Catharine and extended family members walking across the gym floor. Ellyn's visitation was the next day, yet her family knew how much it would mean to my girls that they came to show their support.

(Later after the season had ended, Ernie was asked by a reporter why he went to our matches. His response was, "It was hard being there and supporting them. I knew there were players that were struggling with it [Caroline's and Ellyn's death]. If I could be there, I was going to be there and support the team. I had to be there. Caroline and Ellyn would want me to be there. They wouldn't want me to run away from this scene. I was doing what they wanted me to do. Caroline was a pillar, Ellyn was a wonderful and fantastic person who the whole community enjoyed and appreciated. There's been lots of questions and confusion and lots of good talks and crying and hugging.")

The girls looked at me expectantly. They knew we had a limited time to warm up for the match, but I knew they needed to talk to Ernie more than they needed to warm up.

"Go ahead," I said and watched as they raced over to Ernie. He put his arms around as many of them as possible, and the rest of them made a circle around him and he pulled them all into a tight hug. I could tell he was trying desperately not to cry. When the girls turned away, I saw his shoulders slump as he made his way up to his seat.

Before we started the match, Kevin Geary, Prairie's varsity coach, announced that the four teams in the main gym should make a circle around the center court. He'd called me earlier in the week to ask if I was okay with what would come next: a short program to honor Caroline before the start of the evening matches. I told him it was okay with me, and that the girls would know what to expect.

The teams made a big circle in the center of the gym. There were two teams in the other gym and we stood there for five minutes waiting for them to join us, my players all standing shoulder to shoulder, holding each other's hands, tears running down their faces, some looking up at the ceiling, others hanging their heads, the camera crews and photographers kneeling in front of them, recording their pain.

The other two teams finally came in and completed the circle and Kevin said a few words and then asked for a moment of silence. I thought about our Caroline and offered up a silent prayer: *Please Line, help your friends get through this night and this season. We love you and we miss you.*

The girls wiped away their tears. Before they stepped on the court, the team broke the huddle by counting to nine and yelling 'West.' On the official's signal, the Bettendorf player served the ball and Anna passed a perfect ball to Kelley. Kelley set to Shelly on the far side of the net. Shelly spiked the ball to the floor and I felt instant satisfaction. The girls played with inspiration and enthusiasm, and we won the first set 21-17. The protocol in volleyball is for the teams to switch benches after each game and we got up and started gathering up clothing, clipboards, and water bottles to go to the other bench. Then Scott turned to me.

"What do we do with Line's shoes?" he asked. "If we leave them here, they'll be under Bettendorf's bench. We don't want to do that."

We looked at each other. This was another thing I hadn't thought through.

"I'll tell you what," he said without hesitation. "For all the games this season, I'll just move them to whatever bench we have. It won't be a big deal."

I gratefully acknowledged his suggestion. It seemed like such a simple detail, but I was only beginning to understand how many little details we would have to face this season. Unforeseen decisions that we were going to have to make on the spot.

We won the second game by the same score to win the best-of-three format for that night's tournament and both the starters and reserves leapt into the air on match point. They calmed down enough to shake hands with the Bettendorf squad and then they erupted with emotion again. They cried, hugged, and screamed as only high school girls are capable, and then they raced over to Ernie to celebrate. Scott and I smiled at each other and let them enjoy the moment.

After the season, Eunice said that that match against Bettendorf was one of her top three memories of the season. She talked about how amazing it felt to actually win a game, and most of all, she remembered all of their tears before the match and the smiles they had after the match. That first win gave her hope for the season.

The night wore on and we lost our matches against Pleasant Valley and North Scott. During one critical point in the second set against North Scott, the pressure I was feeling finally got the best of me. On game point, North Scott passed a ball directly above the net and Shelly slammed it back to the floor: an apparent game winner. My girls began to celebrate but the official overturned the call; he said that when Shelly hit the ball it was still on North Scott's side of the net, which is illegal. He gave the point to North Scott and they rallied to win the second set. Those kinds of situations happen all the time in sports. Normally I'd glare at the official and leave it at that, but this time I was out of control. Now instead of winning the match 2 – 0, we were going to have play a third set. I knew my players weren't emotionally or physically capable of playing any more volleyball that evening.

The official got off the ladder and walked across the court toward the team benches, and asked for the captains to join him near the scorer's table for the coin flip to determine serve. I had a total meltdown. I whirled around from my place near our bench and moved to within inches of his face. Making sure no one else could hear me but him, I growled menacingly, "I don't have a captain. She's dead."

Visibly shaken, the official turned to Scott and asked for a captain. Scott looked at me, his blue eyes reflecting his confusion. Seeing that I wasn't going to respond, he sent Shelly over to join the North Scott captain.

I regretted my outburst the moment it happened, and it still bothers me to this day. I shouldn't have lost my composure, especially since I'd vowed to myself that I would be strong for the girls and not allow my emotions to get the best of me under these trying times. I wanted to be their rock, the person they could rely on, and I couldn't even make it through our first night of competition without falling apart. I was embarrassed and disappointed in myself.

Not unexpectedly, North Scott controlled the third set and beat us 15-9. On the bus ride home, I thought about the game. Kelley and Eunice both worked extremely hard at setting and I appreciated their effort. Eunice had been campaigning to be the setter, but she's more valuable to us as a hitter. Kelley still doesn't have a starting role on the team. This is her first season as a varsity player and she's still finding her sea legs, but I liked what I saw of her setting. Eunice did a good job too, but it didn't really work to have two setters.

Right then and there, I made my decision. *We'll go back to a single setter offense for the remainder of the season.* Without consulting Scott, I knew who the setter was going to be.

## CHAPTER 17

# WE NEED A SETTER

We return to the gym to practice. It's the day after Ellyn's visitation. I can tell that my players are emotionally and physically drained. All the seniors look like they're on the verge of tears, which seems like our new normal. Instead of having fun in our practices, my girls are just going through the motions. It feels like we're waiting out a jail sentence.

I've decided that Kelley is going to be our new setter. It will be easier for our hitters to adjust to one setter instead of having two setters rotating in and out every three rotations. In my mind, Kelley's the logical choice. My gut instincts tell me that if anyone can learn the complexities of setting in a short amount of time, it's her. She's a good enough athlete to set in all six rotations, and, more importantly, she's intelligent and will catch on right away to what she'll have to do.

At the start of practice I pull Kelley aside. "Kell, we're going to run a 5-1 offense during the remainder of the season, and you have to be our setter. This will put us in the best position to have some success. I know it'll be hard for you, but I'm confident that you'll be able to do it."

Her jaw muscles tighten and I can see the conflicting emotions etched on her face. She's 5-foot-10, but seems to visibly shrink when she hears my words. I know what she's thinking: *This is Caroline's position. Please don't do this to me.*

Her blue eyes begin to fill with tears. She looks at me and utters, "No."

Line was one of Kelley's best friends since they were little. Caroline had been staying at her family's home the two days before her accident, because Ernie hadn't been comfortable with Caroline staying at the farm alone. He was spending the nights with Ellyn in the hospital, and Aileen Musselman, Ellyn's sister, was driving Catharine to her senior year of college. Kelley had moved her belongings downstairs into a newly remodeled basement, and she and Caroline spent hours down there talking about Ellyn. Kelley had been Caroline's emotional lifeline, holding her when she cried, and listening when she talked. During one particularly rough time for Caroline, Kelley wrote down all the words to "I Won't Let Go" by Rascal Flatts, a hauntingly beautiful song in which the singer pledges to another that he will stand by her, no matter what happens in life. It meant so much to Line that she presented the song lyrics to her mother. I understand that Kelley feels setting for West High will be a tremendous burden, and I wondered, *Am I asking the impossible from her?*

"Listen," I say, grabbing her shoulders gently and pulling her head close to mine. "This is the only option our team has right now. You have to trust me like you've never trusted anyone before. I can get you through this. Trust me, I can train you. Trust me that I won't let you fail. You're the right person for this job. Please promise me that you'll at least try."

She finally looks up at me. "I'll try," she says.

I give her a reassuring hug and call the team over. "You all did a great job last night. I'm so proud of your efforts. Scott and I decided that we need to run a 5-1 offense and that Kelley is going to fill that position."

Fourteen pairs of eyes immediately look over at Kelley to see her reaction. She nervously pushes an errant strand of her long blondish-brown hair away from her face and stares straight ahead, refusing to make eye contact with anyone.

"I expect you to support her and help her with this

transition." I look directly at Shelly and Eunice and continue, "She doesn't need to be perfect in order for us to be successful."

As the players start to partner up for warm-ups I pull Eunice and Shelly aside. "Listen you two, Kelley's going to need a tremendous amount of positive reinforcement as she learns how to set. I don't care if the ball is set ten feet beyond the net, you two need to reassure her that her sets are fine. Great hitters can handle anything, and I need you two to have that mentality. Even if the set results in a hitting error, please take ownership of the error."

Hitters have fragile egos. They never feel like they've been set perfectly enough in a match to execute flawless hits, and they usually blame the setter when things don't go well. These two are the strongest hitters on the team, and the only way Kelley will develop any confidence is if she feels they support her one hundred percent. I'm relieved when they both nod and turn to rejoin their team. I know it won't be this simple, but for now they seem on board.

Kelley's setting tutorial begins. I work with her on one net, and Scott takes the rest of the team to the other net. I have full confidence that Scott can effectively train the rest of the team, as now it's my responsibility to train Kelley. I have my own secret doubts about whether I can do that. Under normal circumstances I spend several years preparing our setters, but now we only have twelve weeks before the state tournament.

I start Kelley with the most basic setter training: simple repetition to work on ball speed and height. I toss her hundreds of balls and she attempts to set them to Cat Rebelskey, a senior who had left the team to be in show choir, but then decided to come back as our team manager after Caroline died. Kelley struggles with even the basics, and I have to remind myself that she's trying to learn a position most athletes begin training for in sixth grade. She's not going to learn this overnight.

She's going to have to learn how to transition off the net, square up to her hitters, and become consistent with ball placement. Once she has a grasp on those skills, we'll begin to tackle running plays and the nuances of reading defenses.

This is probably going to be the most accelerated setter training ever attempted.

Kelley's miserable the entire time. After forty minutes, I can tell that she's had enough. She joins the others, but she still looks despondent. Between drills she stands there with her arms crossed. She doesn't even seem to notice when the other girls encourage her; she looks completely shut down. I've never seen anyone so miserable in my life. I might not be able to cheer her up, but I at least need to get her to relax and not feel so much pressure.

I pull the team together at the end of practice. I turn to Kelley and say, "Listen Kelley, you can do this! Think of me as your BFF. We're going to be inseparable. I've always wanted a seventeen-year-old best friend." The rest of the team begins to smile. Kelley looks at me like I'm crazy, as if she has no idea where I'm going with this. I continue on.

"We'll hang out at the mall, go shopping and *do everything together just like best friends.* In fact, I'll come over to your house for supper tonight. No wait, I have an even better idea…Charlie and I will move into your house *for the rest of the season.*"

I finally get her to smile. The team huddles, then gets ready to go home. Kelley goes to the side of the gym to pick up her equipment and I suddenly have an idea: I'm going to take this even further.

I quickly call Shelly over. "Listen. Call Kelley's mom and explain to her what I just told Kelley. Ask Shirley if she'd mind putting out another place setting for dinner tonight?"

Laughing, Shelly calls Shirley Fliehler, who quickly agrees to set a fourth place setting on the table. I have no intention of going to the Fliehler's tonight, but I can't help smiling all the way home when I imagine Kelley walking into the house and noticing the extra plate. (Shirley will later tell me that Kelley screamed when she saw that fourth plate and said, "Is she really coming *here* for supper?")

It's the following Monday. I teach a physical education class before school and today as soon as the class is over, I walk up the hall to the senior locker area. I talk to Squeaks and Shelly, and wait for Kelley to arrive.

I see her before she sees me and I yell down the hall, "Hello, best friend!"

As soon as Kelley hears me she screams, and hides behind Shelly. We all begin to laugh hysterically, even Kelley. She puts her books in her locker, but continues to maneuver so that Shelly and Squeaks form a barrier between us.

"Don't forget, best friend," I say to Kelley, "I'm going to be everywhere you are!" I hold both my index fingers up in front of my face, parallel and an inch apart. "People are going to say, 'There's Kelley, there's Brez.' 'There's Brez, there's Kelley.'" I dance my hands from side to side.

"Oh my God, that's so creepy," Kelley says with a small smile. She turns and heads off to her first-hour class.

Between first and second period, I walk into her Language Arts classroom and sit at her assigned desk. I can't help but chuckle in anticipation of her arrival. When she walks in the room and sees me sitting in her seat she turns bright red and covers her face with both hands. "This can't be happening," she keeps repeating, to the bemusement of her classmates. I get up, pat her on the shoulder, and leave the classroom. I plan to continue these types of distractions for the remainder of the season. I'll do anything in my power to ease her pain and self-created pressure.

## CHAPTER 18

# FAKE IT TILL YOU MAKE IT

I'm sitting next to Scott in the Xavier High School gym in Cedar Rapids, IA. With a 1-2 record, we've dropped to seventh in the 5A state rankings, while Xavier is ranked sixth in 4A. Schools in Iowa are assigned one of five levels for post-season competition, based on enrollment: 1A are the smallest schools and 5A the largest. Some conferences, such as ours, have schools that fall into different classifications, even though we're in the same league.

I know the girls are apprehensive. The Saints have a talented squad, but that's not the only reason we're struggling. For the fourth time in the first game, Kelley has set an unhittable ball. I watch as she runs under a great pass and oversets a ball that almost hits the score table ten feet away from the court.

"Time out," I say to the official. The girls reluctantly jog over to the side line. "Scott, talk to the rest of the girls."

I motion to Kelley to follow me and I pull her out of the range where others can hear us. "Talk to me Kell. What's going on out there?"

It's obvious that she's flustered and on the verge of tears.

"I'm terrible. I can't do this!" she yells. "Anna is giving me some great passes, but I can't get the ball to the hitters. Have someone else set."

I shake my head. "Kelley, that isn't an option. *You are our setter.* You need to exude confidence and if you don't feel confident, then dang it, fake it till you make it. Your teammates only care that you look in control. As long as you don't externalize your feelings, they'll believe in you. Focus right now on appearing more relaxed. As far as your mechanics, get your feet set under the ball. You are setting on the move. Only worry about that and let me worry about the hitters."

The girls go back out on the court and Scott turns to me questioningly, "Well? Did you settle our setter down?"

"Scott, she's trying to overthink the position. Her only role right now should be to get to the ball and put it in the air in a playable area – nothing else! She's trying to be a leader, role model, and setter. In other words, she's trying to be Caroline. She doesn't need to be Caroline."

Before play resumes, I look up into the stands. Our side of the gym has over two hundred people wearing their bright blue Live Like Line shirts, supporting our team. In past years, we would have about fifty people attend our away matches – usually players' families and a few friends. It's so different to have a crowd attending a volleyball match, and actually cheering the team on. (I find out later that several of our students sent out pleas on social media to encourage their classmates to come to our matches.)

A television camera is behind our endline of the court and another is behind our bench. This match is being aired live on television. For the first time ever, KCRG has added three volleyball matches to its regular season sports package, which normally features football games. Ironically, our team is playing in two of those three featured games. I can't help but wonder if KCRG's decision to schedule us as the featured volleyball team for their television coverage has to do with Caroline's accident? As play is ready to resume, I hear the play-by-play announcer say, "Well hopefully Coach Bresnahan's time out will settle her team down."

I watch as Xavier serves and Squeaks passes Kelley a

great ball. Olivia Fairfield approaches the net for a quick attack and Kelley delivers her a perfect set. The ball slams to the floor and the players yell in excitement. Volleyball is a very emotional sport and players often celebrate after an important point. I know from their reaction that this was a big point for their confidence— Kelley's in particular.

Our play on the court becomes more consistent and soon we win the match, shake hands with the Xavier coaches and players along the net, and then the girls race over to the stands. The students in the crowd leave the bleachers to congratulate the girls on their victory. It's such a nice change to see them happy.

I move back to our bench, sit down on one of the chairs, and I drop my head. It's impossible not to think about how much Caroline would have loved this moment: a nice win, all the fans, and, of course, live television. I can't keep my emotions in check. Scott puts his arm around my shoulder and pulls my head next to his. He doesn't say anything. He doesn't need to, as we both share the same thoughts.

On the bus ride home, the girls enjoy cookies and candy compliments of the Xavier squad. Coach Barb Sullivan and her girls have given us a laundry basket filled with goodies, treats, toys, and hand-written messages of support. I can see Kelley occasionally smile at her teammates' antics, but most of the time she stares out the bus window, lost in thought. I walk to the back seat of the moving bus where she's sitting.

"Move over kiddo," I say and slide into the seat beside her. "You're doing a great job, Kell. I know how hard this is and I'm so proud of you. Hang in there. Trust me when I tell you that setting will become easier."

She nods her head and I put my arm around her, but she continues to stare out at the blackness, lost in her own personal hell.

## CHAPTER 19
# PITY PARTY

It's Labor Day, three weeks after Caroline died, and I'm finishing up making my practice plans in my office. We won the Marshalltown tournament over the weekend, but I wasn't satisfied with our play. We were inconsistent during the morning, but we were still fortunate enough to finish as one of the top two teams and qualify for the championship round. We were marginally better in the semi-finals and championship match, but I knew we weren't playing to our potential.

I walk into the gym and call the players over.

"We need to talk," I tell them. "It's time to start playing quality volleyball. If you think for one moment that teams are going to throw us a pity party because we lost Caroline, you need to think again. You are the defending state champions. Every single team wants to beat you. Do you think when we travel to Cedar Falls tomorrow night that they'll take it easy on you because we have heavy hearts? We need to start playing with energy, passion, and excitement. It's time to start playing like a West High volleyball team."

This is the first time I've even raised my voice since Caroline died, let alone said anything stern or critical of the girls' listless efforts. The girls look at each other and I can tell I've gotten their attention. The team jogs off to warm up and Scott turns to me and grins. "Welcome back!"

His comment gives me pause. How can I expect my

girls to give me more effort when I've been subdued and not pushing them to work harder? I haven't helped them to improve, I've just been going through the motions myself.

Before I can respond to Scott, the gym is suddenly filled with loud music. I turn around and watch as Kelley adjusts the speaker volume even higher—the same as Caroline used to do—before jogging off to join her teammates. I'm so proud she's taken ownership of a task that used to be Line's. This tells me that she's starting to assume a leadership role on the team. She's morphing into a setter. I've been wondering if we'd have music playing in our gym this season—I had my doubts. Caroline was all about music and dancing, and the girls had seemed hesitant to turn the music back on now that she's gone. The silence during warm-ups has been deafening.

We've lost so many things with Line's death, but now at least we have music again. I'm sure most people wouldn't think the lack of warm-up music was a big deal, but it seemed significant to me. We've broken through one emotional barrier.

The girls practice hard and the music plays for the full ninety minutes. Normally we'd turn the music off once the warm-ups were complete, but this is a breakout day. I know I need to cut them a little slack.

The girls are laughing and in great spirits as they walk out of the gym at the end of practice. Kelley's the last to leave because she's taken the time to put the stereo system away.

"Hey, Kell," I yell across the gym. "Could you pick out some better music tomorrow, and for heaven's sake, *turn down the volume.*"

She looks at me for a moment and then a grin lights up her face—she knows I said this to Caroline at least three times a week.

"Yeah, maybe. But I don't think I have any music that's from your junior prom in 1923!"

She turns and runs out of the gym before I can come up with a biting retort to her insult.

## CHAPTER 20

# LIVE LIKE LINE: DETERMINATION

It's 3:30 on Tuesday, September 6, and we're on the bus to Cedar Falls. It's our third conference match of the season and our first one playing a 5A-ranked team. We usually take a yellow school bus to our away matches, but because it's a two-hour trip on a school night, I've decided to take $300 out of our volleyball account to pay extra for a charter bus. It's a much more comfortable ride and the kids are able to study on the way home—they can't do that on the yellow bus because it has no lights.

I'm sitting in the front seat with Scott, and our sophomore coach, Ashten. The sophomore players are sitting in the seats directly behind us, and the varsity players occupy the back half of the bus. The girls have been very subdued during the first ninety minutes of the trip. I turn in my seat to look around and see what the players are doing to occupy their time. Some of them are doing schoolwork, a few are still eating lunch, but most of them are sitting silently in their seats with their eyes closed.

For the past few years, Caroline always brought a movie that we'd put in the DVD player and watch during the long trips. She and I had an on-going feud as to what was an appropriate movie. I demanded that the movie be PG-13, but she always tried to slip an R-rated movie past me. Last year I made her open her backpack so I could see what DVDs she brought for our trip to Dubuque. She sheepishly handed me the movie Hangover and I made her take it back into school and put it in her locker. The memory of her mischievous grin in that moment gives me pause.

I turn back around in my seat and Scott, sensing my mood, grins and says, "If it was this quiet any other year, we would have known that Caroline was up to something."

"My God, you've got that right," I reply. I force myself to smile. I know Scott is trying to cheer me up, and I realize I need to do the same thing for my players. If we walk into the gym in this mood we'll get trounced. "I think I'll roam to the back to make sure there's no Icy Hot back there."

We both grin.

Using the backs of the seats for support, I carefully make my way towards the rear of the bus. The vehicle's swaying makes it difficult to navigate the maze of gym bags tossed in the center aisle.

Squeaks and Anna are sitting together sharing a single set of earbuds plugged into an iPod, and Shelly and Kelley are four seats behind them, all the way in the back. Anna's leaning her head against the seat, listening to music with her eyes closed. This is nothing out of the ordinary. Anna's a first-generation American; she goes to Russia with her mom every summer to visit her grandparents. On the court she's our most fiery player, but off the court she's reserved, and doesn't create drama or conflicts like other teenage girls. But it's unusual to see Squeaks, Shelly, and Kelley sitting in their seats doing nothing. Normally Shelly would be standing in the aisle gyrating, pouring water on someone's head or emitting impressive burps, and Squeaks and Kelley would be screaming in response, egging her on.

In that moment it comes to me that I'm going to have to let down my own barriers even more this season than

I already have. Being goofy and doing things I normally wouldn't do will help change their focus. I'm going to have to let the girls see that I'm vulnerable. And I'm going to do anything I can to make them laugh, including being the brunt of their jokes. In past seasons, I didn't mind getting teased by the girls, but there was a time and a place to goof around. This year, I'm going to give them all the latitude they need, even if it takes away from our practice time.

I plop down on Squeaks, half sitting on top of her. "Have you guys been missing me?" I ask with a manic smile on my face.

"Oh my God, you are such a creeper," Squeaks yells, feigning horror as I bully my way deeper into the seat bench.

Anna doesn't say a word but looks at me like I'm certifiably crazy, the way she always does when I act impulsively or do something out of the ordinary.

I pull the earbud from Squeaks' ear and put it into my own. I don't recognize the song, but that doesn't stop me from throwing my arms in the air and dancing to the beat. I pull out the ear bud and hand it back to Squeaks. I begin to stand up and the other varsity girls smile nervously, unsure what I might do next.

"Where's my best friend?" I say loudly.

Kelley screams, "No!"

I run past the final four rows and throw myself across Kelley and Shelly's laps. I grab Kelley's pillow, turn onto my back, put my feet up on the back of the seat in front of us and pretend to fall asleep. Shelly and Kelley begin to pummel me with their fists and attempt to push me off the seat, but I use the seat in front of us for leverage to stay in place. After a minute or so, I jump up without saying a word and make my way back to the front of the bus. When I reach my seat, Scott looks at me, smiles, and shakes his head as if he can't believe what he's just witnessed. Still, I can tell he knew exactly what my intention was.

We reach Cedar Falls High School and the players head to the locker room to change. Scott, Ashten, and I walk into the gym. We're arranging our clipboards and stat sheets at our bench area when I feel a tap on my shoulder. It's Matt Flaherty, Cedar Falls' head coach.

He pulls me into a giant bear hug. "Oh Kathy, I'm so sorry. Words can't begin to express how badly I feel for you and your girls. If there's anything I can do for you, please know you can count on me."

I've always liked Matt. He's a genuinely kind man and our teams have had some great matches in the past. I know he's sincere, but I also know that his concern hasn't affected his attitude toward the upcoming match. His team will be well -prepared to pull off the upset. His team is ranked seventh in the state and we're ranked sixth. I know there's nothing he wants more than to beat us tonight.

"Thanks, my friend," I say.

We wish each other good luck and I sit down on the bleachers behind our bench. The gym is quickly filling with excited Cedar Falls' students and fans—this is their conference home opener. Cameramen are setting up their equipment on the endlines of the court and up above us in the balcony area. I forgot that tonight's match was going to be televised live. The various media outlets—newspapers, television and radio—continue to keep the public updated on our volleyball team's success. Whenever I read or watch yet another story featuring the team, I feel like a scab is being pulled off a wound. We already have enough emotional triggers without external reminders.

About thirty minutes before our match should begin, eight West High students walk in, six girls and two boys, all wearing jeans and blue Live Like Line t-shirts. They look around the gym casually, as if this is just another ordinary game. I recognize Danielle Chelf and Lauren Larson, but it's hard to make out the other six. I can't believe they all drove two hours on a school night just to watch their friends play volleyball. In the past, only the parents of the players ever bothered to travel this far. Lauren's a West High junior who used to play volleyball, but now focuses on softball. I've always seen her cheering on the team at home matches, but never when we've played outside Iowa City. Danielle's a senior who played basketball with Shelly and Caroline last year. She's good friends with all my senior players.

Lauren comes over to me and I give her a hug. "What are you guys doing here?"

"We're not going to miss a match all season, Brez. These are our friends and they need us." She swipes at tears, looks over at Shelly, and gives her a thumbs-up.

I watch her cross back to the other side of the gymnasium and my vision blurs with my own tears.

Scott's on the court running warm-up drills with the varsity players, and I'm at the score table turning in our starting lineup with my back to the players. So I don't see what my girls see, but I hear their excited screams, "Ernie!"

I look around and sure enough, Ernie's walking across the floor, his thinning gray hair matted with perspiration. His 6-foot-5 frame dwarfs his friend Paul Etre, who is eleven inches shorter. They're both wearing their Live Like Line shirts. Paul's an administrator in Ernie's surgical unit at the hospital, and the two men have been inseparable since the accident.

The West players run over to greet Ernie. They take turns giving and receiving hugs from him. He towers above them and has to bend down to greet them. All the girls are smiling from ear to ear. They resume their warm-ups more energetically. Ernie looks across the court and gives me a small, sad smile. He looks tired and I can see that he's lost a great deal of weight. I can't imagine how emotionally difficult it must be for him to be here, but here he is. I return his smile and touch my hand to my heart to let him know how much this means to us. I'm awed by his strength and determination to support my players. I'm so grateful that he still wants to be a part of our lives.

My players dominate the first set by a score of 25 – 14. I can tell that they're fueled by the fact that their friends and Ernie are here. But the problem with starting off a game on an emotional high is that it's difficult to maintain the intensity for the duration of a match. I never want my players to be too high or too low emotionally. It's fun while the roller coaster is at the apex of the ride but eventually the cars begin that stomach-lurching downward plunge, and my heart sinks and my stomach clenches as I watch my team start to unravel midway through the second set.

We begin to make unforced errors. Our serves are going out-of-bounds or in the net. Kelley is still struggling in the setting position, so our timing is off for our hitters. Shelly hits several balls out-of-bounds, and Eunice and Hannah are only attempting off-speed tips. The Cedar Falls players quickly adjust their defense to pick up these easy hits, and their offense begins to take control of the game with big hits that we can't dig up. Our eight-point lead disintegrates and we barely hold on for a 25 – 23 win. The Cedar Falls players, sensing our vulnerability, become more energized and excited. I know they're going to ride that momentum into the third set.

Our hitters—unsure of where Kelley's set will be placed—become hesitant on their approaches. The Russian and Squeaks aren't calling out the Cedar Falls blocker locations to our hitters, so our hitters are hitting directly into blocks and the Cedar Falls front court begins to dominate the net. Kaz Brown, Cedar Fall's six-foot-four sophomore middle blocker, stuff-blocks Eunice, slamming her hit straight back across the net and onto the floor, then turns to her teammates and screams. In one quick movement, she turns back to the net and screams again, jabbing her finger at my players.

I'm furious that she's taunting my girls. But of course

I keep my feelings bottled up. I understand that she's using her emotions to fuel her own teammates.

Kaz gets five kills and three blocks to lead Cedar Falls to a 25 – 20 win in the third set. I can feel the momentum and the match slipping away from us. I turn in our line-up for the fourth set and join my girls in the huddle. I'm not even sure what to say to them right now. It seems as if they've used up whatever energy reserves they might have had.

Scott shoots me a questioning look and I shake my head slightly: I don't have the answers. He turns to the players. "#&%&% them," he says. "Go out and play West High volleyball."

I'm shocked and so are the girls. We've never heard Scott swear before. Normally I'm the loud one in the huddle, and he's more even-keeled. I see surprise register in my players' faces and then they look at each other, chuckling. Scott frowns and looks up into the bleachers where the television commentators are sitting. He shakes his head in resignation and puts his hand out to end our huddle; it's apparent he isn't going to say anything else. The girls lay their hands over his and we all count to nine and yell, "West!"

We break from the huddle and the girls run back out to the court, snapped out of their stupor. They begin to serve, pass, and hit like a different team than they have during the past two sets. The Cedar Falls players, especially Kaz, seem shocked by our renewed passion. The expressions on their faces and their slumped shoulders show me that they've gotten the message that this game belongs to us. We completely outplay them for the remainder of the set and decisively beat them 25 – 13. In the final play of the match, Kaz rises up to attempt a kill in the middle of the court. Eunice times her block perfectly and stuffs the ball back to Cedar Falls. The rest of our players yell and run over to congratulate her, but Eunice simply turns toward our bench with a slight grin and gives Scott a thumbs-up.

Scott and I join our girls and we form a line and head to the net. The Cedar Falls players' form their own line and approach the net from the other direction. We all hold out our right hands and slap each player coming toward us, saying, "Good game, good game, good game." But when I hold out my hand to Kaz she pulls hers back. I'm confused – did she do that on purpose? I keep walking, slapping the next girl's hand and saying, "Good game."

After we go through the line I turn to Scott. "I'm not sure what that '#&%&%' them' was all about, but feel free to jump in any time," I say to him with my usual good-humored sarcasm. "Next time, though, don't hold back. Make sure you tell us how you *really* feel."

Scott grins at me. I always chastise the girls about using inappropriate language—if someone drops the f-bomb in practice, the entire team has to run sprints. Squeaks in particular always fakes dropping the f-bomb, just to get my reaction. There have been several times this season that she's jokingly responded to something I've said with "What the fffffff....." She doesn't finish the word, but it doesn't matter. As soon as I hear her drag out the letter 'F,' I send the team to the sideline to run. I don't expect Scott to swear either, but in this instance it seemed appropriate and it worked.

Scott, Ashten and I get on the bus ahead of our players. The girls eventually finish up in the locker room and as they file past me on the bus, I give each of them a high five. I can tell by their smiles that they're happy with the win and I'm pleased with how they responded to adversity.

Squeaks is the last to board. I extend my hand to her and she slaps it hard.

"Stay in your seat on the trip home!" she says, giving me a mischievous grin.

# CHAPTER 21

# THE CAROLINE FOUND
# EXTRAVAGANZA

We compete in a tournament almost every Saturday, from Labor Day weekend to mid-October, with only two weekends off. Each tournament is hosted by a different school. It's fairly common that we leave for away tournaments at 6:00 a.m. and arrive home after 8:00 p.m. If we make it to the championship match of the tournament, the girls will have played six matches and as many as eighteen games or sets. Saturday tournaments are long and grueling, but the girls fill their breaks with dancing and a great deal of laughter. Last week, the first tournament of the year, we were in Marshalltown. Today we're here at West.

I arrive at school at 7:00 a.m., pull into a parking space, get out, and walk across the blacktop. Already the humidity seems to hang in the air. When I open the gym doors, it feels like a furnace blast hitting my face. It's going to be a long, energy-sapping day. This is the twentieth year that we've held the West High Extravaganza—a twelve-team tournament involving some of the best teams in the state. The whole thing takes about ten hours if we're lucky.

I don't harbor any illusions that we'll win the championship today. History tells me otherwise. We've made it into the finals of the West-High-hosted tournament seven times, but we've never won. Three times the Wahlert team, coached by Tom Keating, beat us for the title.

We didn't get home Tuesday night until almost midnight, and the girls have been lethargic in practices for the past three days. It's going to be a long day.

The tournament involves three pools with four teams each. The teams are ranked, or seeded, based on their records and state rankings. The goal is to try to ensure that all the pools are equally strong. So, for example, we'd never be in the same pool as Dubuque Wahlert, which is ranked number one among schools of their size, since we're ranked number one among the schools of our size—the large schools—and putting our two teams in the same pool would make that particular pool stronger than the others. After all of these matches, the top eight teams—based on their records for the day— play each other, and any team that loses is eliminated. At the same time the four teams with the worst record after pool play have a consolation championship.

Twenty minutes before the start of the first game, the coaches and officials gather in the team room to cover the rules of the tournament today. Marv Reiland, our athletic director, walks to the front to address us. While he waits for all the coaches to arrive, he hands out two meal tickets to everyone, to cash in during the day at the concession stand. The last couple of coaches wander in. Everyone's wearing the requisite coaching apparel of khaki shorts and polo shirts, except for me and Scott— we've got on our blue Live Like Line t-shirts. There are twenty coaches and eight officials here today. The officials are all sitting by themselves on folding chairs over near the table holding the doughnuts, and most of us coaches are standing around the room talking to each other. We don't see each other that often and when we do we catch up and commiserate about team drama or parent problems—both inherent when coaching girls. My friend Jan Thyne, the coach at Wahlert, is one of the last people to enter the room, and she finds me among the group and hugs me. She hasn't seen me since the accident though she's sent emails and texts and a card from her team.

Marv waits till everyone in the room gets quiet, clears his throat, and begins. "I want to thank all of you for coming today to the Caroline Found Extravaganza. I know you're all familiar with the tragedy that struck our school a month ago, and I also know that many of you have reached out to offer your support during this most difficult of times. Brez and I decided that a wonderful way to recognize Caroline would be to rename the tournament in her honor. I hope your teams enjoy today as much as she would have. The quality of play should be exceptional and I look forward to watching all of your teams compete."

I'm not sure that we have the stamina to be competitive today and my only hope is that we won't get eliminated early from our own tournament or, God forbid, have to play in the consolation bracket. I know how bad my players will feel if that happens. This tournament today is personal for them. It represents Caroline to them—not only in name but in their hearts. Line loved playing every Saturday, but her enthusiasm was immeasurable when it came to playing this particular tournament at home. Her family always attended and we always had many more supporters on this day, the second Saturday of September, than at any other regular-season Saturday tournament. This is also the day when the University of Iowa football team plays Iowa State here in Iowa City. Their one o'clock kick-off happens right at the end of our pool play and the concurrence of the volleyball and football games is a two-edged sword. On one hand it creates a lot of bad traffic—there have been times that some teams have arrived late because of the traffic jam exiting the interstate. The football stadium is located only a mile away on the same street as our high school. But on the other hand, there's a lot of extra excitement among our fans and extra attendees at our games, as alumni and other people from out of town who wouldn't come otherwise, stop by to watch some volleyball before heading to the college football game.

We begin pool play against North Cedar, a small school with only 300 students located thirty miles north of Iowa City. North Cedar has a competitive volleyball program but with an enrollment difference of 1500 students, this normally wouldn't be an even match-up. Today is different.

We are easily scoring points against North Cedar, but none of my players seem excited after a big point. Normally they'd run together and clap their hands in unison at the end of a play but today they're silent; they're acting as if volleyball is a nine-to-five job instead of a sport they love. We win the first set by a wide margin, 21 – 7. But it's not so much that we're dominating—it's more that North Cedar seems intimidated to be playing us. I can tell they aren't trying to win the match as much as trying to survive by returning our serves and hits directly back over the net to our side.

As the second set gets going, the North Cedar players appear to gain more confidence as they sense my girls' ambivalence about the contest. The North Cedar girls get louder after they earn a point or when we make a hitting or serving error. We aren't passing the ball well or communicating on the court. When a volley ball team stops talking to each other during play, you're in trouble. Everything seems to be a struggle for our defense as well as offense. We just can't get into the flow of the game and we're lucky to win 21 – 15.

The next two matches, against Mt. Vernon and Davenport North, play out the same way. We win the opening set easily, but barely hold on to win the second match. It seems like my players don't have the wherewithal to compete today. We're having difficulty receiving serves, so our passes are off the net. Kelley's struggling with her setting. With poor sets, our hitters are having difficulty putting any shots down to the floor.

When our pool play ends, we have a half hour break because the other two pools are still playing. The girls go to the team room to munch on the food their parents have brought in, and Scott and I stay out in the gym to scout the teams that we may be playing in the championship bracket. After taking a few notes, I turn to Scott. "Any suggestions as to how we can get them focused? We're going to get our butts kicked in the quarterfinals if we continue to play like this."

Scott looks straight ahead. "I don't think there's anything we can do. It's up to them. They have to be able to figure it out on the court. At some point, someone's going to have to emerge as a floor leader, but right now we don't have that person. Until that happens, we're going to struggle. But I think they'll start to play better this afternoon."

"I hope you're right," I say. "Maybe I'm expecting too much from them this soon." Tomorrow it'll be exactly one month since the accident.

It's not the winning that's important to me. I just want my players to feel like they're accomplishing something positive. I know that for some of them, like Hannah Infelt, volleyball has become a job. I can tell she's playing with grim determination to do well for Caroline's sake, but volleyball itself isn't giving her any pleasure. For Kelley, the responsibility of being the setter is weighing heavily. I can see it in her body language when she doesn't do well. I know it's my responsibility to help each of the girls reach their goal of winning a state title. But with the way we're playing, that goal seems impossible. At this point I'll be satisfied if volleyball is an avenue for healing, rather than an emotional struggle.

But Scott was right that once we started the championship play we'd do better. No casual observer would have watched us and said that we were extremely talented or that we were overpowering our opponents, but the girls played just well enough to win every game.

It was almost as if they knew they had limited energy and were using just as much energy as they needed to.

We beat Waterloo Columbus 25 - 17 and 25 – 14 in the quarterfinals. Shelly was pounding some big kills and the most pleasant surprise offensively was Laynie Whitehead. Our ninth grader was really starting to look comfortable on the court. She had some nice hits and she fully utilized her six-foot-one frame as a blocker.

We beat Pella Christian 25 – 20 and 25 -19 in the semifinals, thanks to Eunice and Hannah controlling the net. With both of them over six foot tall, the smaller Pella players had to finesse their attacks to get around our blocks, and the Russian and Squeaks did a great job picking up the off-speed hits.

Now we're in the middle of the final match of the day, playing Dubuque Wahlert, the top-ranked 3A team in the state, for the tournament championship. Our two teams have split the first two sets and the tournament championship has come down to this game. The last game of the tournament takes only fifteen points to win. Right now, we're tied at 7 – 7.

Neither of our teams has been able to make a run and seize the momentum. It's like two heavy-weight boxers in the ninth round standing toe-to-toe. Our team delivers a strong uppercut—a floor-rattling spike—only to have Wahlert come back with a right hook—an ace serve—that connects to the jaw.

My players seem to have more confidence, though. I don't know if it's because they're excited to be playing for the championship, or if they're getting more comfortable on the court. I know that if Caroline were here in this moment, she'd be busy rallying her teammates, addressing each player individually, saying exactly what that person needed to hear. She'd push Shelly, saying, "Shelly, you need to hit the ball harder." She'd encourage Laynie and Hannah Infelt, who are more inexperienced, telling them things like, "Don't worry, you'll get it next time." With Squeaks, who gets down on herself whenever she makes an error, Caroline would throw up her hands and say something like, "I don't need a perfect pass, I can get to anything you give me."

Caroline really was a consummate leader. I've never seen anyone else do that so successfully, and not just on the court. She did it everywhere—whether it was creating an impromptu get-together, or setting up a study session after school, or turning some ordinary day into a theme day—she could get anybody to do anything. People wanted to be around her. And now everyone, her teammates most of all, seems rudderless without her.

No one on the team has emerged as a court leader in her absence. Maybe they're afraid to take on that responsibility. Eunice, Shelly, and Anna Pashkova have had all moments where they stepped forward as leaders, but I want to see someone assume that role full time, during practice, in competition, and during off-the-court activities. My hope of hopes is that that person will eventually be Kelley. As setter, she's in the most natural position to be the leader.

Today the championship game doesn't end at fifteen points. A team has to have a two-point lead to win, even if they get to fifteen points, and so far both teams have only managed to lead by one point. Four times, one team has been a point away from winning but the other team tied it up. Finally, with the score 18 - 17, Shelly goes back to serve. Her jump serve is picture perfect and the Wahlert defender is lucky to get to the ball. The ball ricochets off her arms straight above the net where Eunice is waiting like a child anticipating Christmas morning. She times her jump perfectly and slams the overpassed ball straight to the floor on the Wahlert side of the court.

Anna and Squeaks both jump into the air as the ball hits the floor. The Russian yells out a scream and our bench clears as the substitutes rush the floor and hug the starters.

As soon as we shake hands with the Wahlert players, my girls rush over to Marv to get their championship medals. Their laughter fills the air. Scott and I call the girls over to the side of the court to take pictures. Everyone poses playfully for all the parents and grandparents proudly clicking away with their phones and cameras.

I'm so happy for my team. But my eyes are drawn to Caroline's jersey, held up proudly by Squeaks and the Russian, who are kneeling at the front of the group. Line would have just loved being a part of the first West High team ever to win this tournament on our home turf. Right now she would have been kneeling front and center, mugging for the camera and holding her medal up, in the exact spot where her jersey is today. The sight of that jersey gives me a hollow pit in my stomach.

## CHAPTER 22
# "SWEET CAROLINE"

We're in the team room, minutes away from the start of our home opener against Cedar Rapids Prairie. The girls are making faces at each other and screwing around. I try to get them to focus on the match. I can't be angry at them because I know they're acting like this out of nervousness. I feel nervous too. Our student body and many community members have come to this match to support our team, and I'm not sure how we'll respond on the court.

I give up trying to talk to them. Scott and I leave the training room so the girls can do their "secret team dance" before the contest. The West High girls' volleyball team has been doing this ever since anybody can remember. They make up a dance every year to some song on the radio and then they spend ten minutes doing it, all on their own in the locker room—or in the back gym or a hallway or the team room, depending on where we are—before every game. Once last year, Scott and I tried to sneak in and watch them dance, but we were promptly kicked out.

Scott and I step into the gym and I'm amazed by the crowd. Six hundred students fill one side of the gym, and almost every one of them is wearing a Live Like Line t-shirt. The opposite side of the gym is just as full, mostly with people I've never seen at one of our matches: West volleyball alumni, members of St. Andrew's church, complete strangers. Most of them are also wearing Live Like Line shirts. It's by far the largest crowd we've ever had.

I watch some West High senior girls unfurl a large banner in front of the entryway. I can see my players jumping and yelling in the hallway as they wait for the music to start—the song "Bring 'Em Out," by the rapper T.I., is the signal for their entrance into the gym. The song starts, Anna breaks through the banner followed closely behind by her teammates, and the fans roar in unison.

I turn to Scott. "This is unbelievable! It feels like an Iowa football game."

He nods his head in agreement. "I just hope they're ready to play and not worried about the student section."

The teams begin to warm up. Both teams ball-handle on separate sides of the net, then Prairie gets the net for seven minutes while our girls stand to the side, then we get the net for seven minutes. Two minutes before the start of the match, the starters from both teams move to stand on their respective endlines for introductions. I knew we had to recognize Caroline in some manner, so I've given Gary Neuzil, our announcer, a statement. He reads it now.

"Welcome, volleyball fans," he begins. "Tonight's game is a mixture of emotions as we step into the gym for our very first MVC home match without number 9. Caroline was a terrific volleyball player and teammate, but more importantly, she was a remarkable person, reaching out to everyone around her. As you wear those Live Like Line t-shirts in her honor, we ask that you embrace those virtues that made her so special: her generosity, her empathy, her goofy sense of humor and, above all, her passion for life. As a team, we would like to thank everyone, including Cedar Rapids Prairie, for their support, prayers, and words of encouragement. Instead of the customary moment of silence, the West High volleyball team requests that everyone embrace the true sense of Caroline Found by taking a moment to introduce yourself to someone you don't know."

I watch strangers shake hands or embrace, and my emotional Irish side takes over. My eyes fill with tears as everyone in the gym walks around, introducing themselves to someone new. I walk over and hug the Prairie coaches, thank them, and return to our bench area.

The crowd returns to their seats. Ashten Stelken, our sophomore coach, turns to me and grins broadly. "Line would love every minute of this."

The match begins. Before long, we assert our dominance. With four players over six feet tall, our team controls the hitting and blocking at the net, and Kelley does a very good job of running fast tempo sets. The Prairie girls play hard, but they're overmatched and we win the match three sets to none.

The two teams shake hands and then our players mill around on the court. They seem unsure of what to do next, whether to come over to the bench and talk to the coaches as is customary, or run over to the crowd and celebrate. I've already made the decision for them. I look over at Gary and nod. He turns on the stereo and Neil Diamond's "Sweet Caroline" begins to play through the loud speakers. The students rush out of the bleachers and surround the players in the middle of the court. People cry, laugh, and sing at the top of their lungs. Ashten, Scott, and I stand there watching. The adult fans are celebrating up in the bleachers. (From now on, for the remainder of the season, we'll play this song at the conclusion of every match and it will be played at every West High home sporting event during the rest of the school year. It will become a symbol of everything that had happened and is happening now: of Caroline and how we lost her and how we were trying to continue on without her. It's rather ironic that I chose this song because Line hated Sweet Caroline.)

I turn to my two coaches. "Do you realize what's going on? This team represents Caroline and Ellyn to this school and community. Supporting the West High volleyball team is helping everyone with their grief."

They nod in agreement. As Scott, Ashten, and I clear our belongings off the bench, I watch the girls crying and laughing with their friends and families. I worry about the pressure that these girls are going to be under for the remainder of the season to succeed for the droves of people who are coming to their matches.

# CHAPTER 23

# OUR ROLES

**M**y players are emotionally fragile. Every player is reacting differently to our tragedy.

Hannah Infelt has always been a kind and compassionate person. Now, in practices, she lashes out angrily at teammates and coaches. I know this is not personal, but I worry about how it affects the rest of the team. I've started telling her to rate her emotional state at the beginning of each practice, on a scale of one to ten. If she's an eight or nine, I treat her with kid gloves during the whole practice. So far she's never been a ten, but if she ever is, I plan to call her mom and send Hannah home. Most days she's a five or six. The rating system is helping both of us—it gives her a way to verbalize how she feels, and it helps me be sensitive about her behavior, which in any other year I would have considered disrespectful.

Shelly has always had a great sense of humor but was generally over-shadowed by Caroline's outrageousness. Now she has taken on the role as team comedian. One day in early September she hid in the upper bleachers during practice. I looked around for her impatiently—I was trying to get the team to focus and have a productive practice—we hadn't really had one so far this year. As soon as I saw Shelly's blond ponytail sticking up above the risers, I pulled the team to the sidelines and made them start running sprints. She quickly realized what was happening and scampered down from the bleachers to join her teammates as they ran, but I stopped her and made her watch them run for the next several minutes. On another day, she convinced the whole team to hide behind three large wooden boxes we keep in the gym—the girls stand on them during practice to work on arm swing without jumping. The boxes were leaning against the wall that day, and Shelly got everyone to hide inside them. It took Scott and me five minutes to figure out where they were. We finally figured it out because we could hear them giggling. We took some half-empty water bottles out of the trash, walked over to the boxes, and poured the water into the boxes through holes at the top. We held the boxes against the walls so the girls couldn't escape until we let them out. They came out, wet and laughing and mortified that we'd splashed them with *used* water. They had to wear their wet clothes for the entire practice.

It hasn't been easy for our underclassmen to be members of the team this season. If Line was around she would have made them feel comfortable on a senior-dominated team, but in her absence, no one else has stepped in to assist them. In fact, almost the opposite has occurred; the seniors often shut themselves off from the freshmen, sophomores, and juniors on the team. They are protective of their grief and seem to resent the idea that anyone else shares their sense of loss. I don't know how to help the underclassmen feel more welcome by the other girls.

Kelley's the one I worry about the most. She's withdrawn and never enjoys practices like she used to. She doesn't talk; when the other girls are having fun, she stands alone looking solemn, and she often looks like she's on the verge of tears. I continue to work with her one-on- one for forty-five minutes at the start of every practice.

Kelley told me that she's taking out her anger and frustration on her parents, and that when she goes home at night she refuses to talk to them about volleyball or setting in particular. She eats supper and then withdraws to her room for the remainder of the night. Kelley refuses to sleep in her basement bedroom since the accident, choosing instead to sleep next to her mom, just like a frightened child.

I've told the team repeatedly that they can't win for Caroline; they have to play with her passion for the game. But I know they're still thinking *we have to do this for Caroline.* So a few days ago, on September 12, I made the decision that it was time to add some pressure during practice. Most seasons we have this kind of practice several times a week. This season we haven't even had one practice like that.

It's very easy to add stress and pressure to any volleyball drill. For example, I might tell the players they have to get thirty perfect serve receptions in five minutes or they'll have to run sprints. This is an easy drill, until you add consequences or time constraints. Without those the girls can finish this drill in less than five minutes, maybe three. With the pressure of those stressors, they sometimes fall apart. The point is to let them learn how to play under pressure, to have pressure become normal so that when they're about to serve in a big game, they stay calm. Today I tell them they have to do thirty passes in five minutes or they'll have to run sprints. Yesterday, without the pressure of the sprint consequences, they did the drill in five minutes perfectly. Today they fail miserably. Four times they attempt to complete the drill and four times they fail and have to go to the side line to run.

Midway through the fourth set of sprints, Kelley runs off the court in tears.

"Squeaks, go outside and see if Kelley's all right," I say.

Squeaks, more than happy to quit running, leaves and the team fails to complete the drill one more time. When they line up on the sideline, Hannah Infelt steps out, grabs me by the shoulders and stares at me defiantly.

"I'll do whatever you ask," she yells through her tears. "But I need a different reason to be running these sprints than just Caroline. Right now I hate volleyball. *Promise* me that we'll win state."

The entire team stops and waits for my reaction. I put my hands on Hannah's shoulders and look her in the eyes and I tell her the only thing I can think to say, even though I believe it's a lie, "Hannah, I promise you that we'll win state." And then I say, "Everyone take a break and go get a drink of water."

With a heavy heart, I walk outside to see how Kelley's doing.

Kelley's sitting on the ground under a large blue spruce behind the gym. She's crying inconsolably. Squeak's sitting beside her with her arm around her. I sit down beside Kelley. "Kelley, tell me what's going on."

She stops sobbing, but continues to breathe in long gasping breaths. She doesn't say anything for several minutes. Then, without lifting her head from her knees, she blurts out, "I can't do this. I know everyone looks to the setter for leadership and to provide energy. But I don't have that to give. It takes everything I have to even get through school acting normal. By the time I get to practice, I don't have anything left. I'm giving you everything I have!"

"Kelley, look at me," I say.

She lifts her head and looks at me.

"Kelley," I say. "You can't do everything. Each person on the team needs to assume different responsibilities. Your only responsibility is to be the best possible setter that you can be."

She drops her head back down to her knees. I walk back into the gym and ask Scott to bring the rest of the players out. We all sit on the ground near Kelley. I look around at each of the players, and then I ask Kelley to repeat to the team what she has just told me. She refuses.

"Kelley, it's important that you share your feelings

with the rest of the team. Please?"

Finally she repeats what she's just said to Squeaks and me. "I can't do this. I'm putting on an act for eight hours at school. When I get to practice, I have nothing left to give."

There's a stunned silence. Squeaks finally breaks it.

"Kelley," she whispers. "We don't expect you to be Caroline. You're doing such a great job running the offense. We need to all start taking ownership of this season. Please don't think you have to do it all."

The players nod their heads in agreement. The girls all stand up, and Kelley is quickly ensconced in the arms of her friends. Then they brush the pine needles off their spandex shorts and start to walk back in the gym. I stop them before they get to the court and call off the rest of practice—it's clear to me that nothing more will be accomplished in the gym today—and the girls gratefully head off to the parking lot.

The Found family (l-r): Ellyn, Catharine, Caroline, Gregg, and Ernie.

The Found family outside Roger Dean Stadium in Jupiter, FL –
Spring Training home of the St. Louis Cardinals.

2010 starting line-up introductions. Line's first season as our starting setter.

No one enjoyed playing volleyball more than Line. The smile never left her face.

Line entertaining her father and friends with the surprises she received from her "Secret Sis" before the match.

A happy state champion.

2010 State Champions

Our team, as well as teams from across the state of Iowa, came to pay their respects during Caroline's visitation which was held in the West High gym due to the large number of people.

This small tree became a memorial to Line and a place of mourning and gathering for the community.

I never ever thought I would have to eulogize one of my players. My final words to the congregation, "Number 9, we'll make you proud."

The theme for our 2011 poster, Remember Us, took on an entirely different meaning than we first intended. Caroline's picture was photo-shopped into the group.

The shoes that Line dedicated to her mother were always put under the first chair on our bench for every match.

The first home match of 2011. Note Ernie in the background in his Live Like Line shirt along with my assistant Scott Sanders.

There was a moment of silence for Caroline before the match. I'm not sure how Olivia, Kelley and Shelly kept it together.

Celebrating a win to the song "Sweet Caroline" became a new tradition.

No one was stronger than Ernie Found. As difficult as it had to be for him, he came to every single match to support us. Here Shelly Stumpff and Olivia Fairchild give him a hug after we won the Spike.

Celebrating a big point in the state championship match against City High.

Kelley runs the offense in the championship match just as Line had one year earlier. She was reluctant to replace Line as setter, but we wouldn't have repeated as State Champions without her.

The joy of winning quickly turned to feelings of relief, guilt, and grief for many of the girls. Here I do my best to console Olivia Mekies.

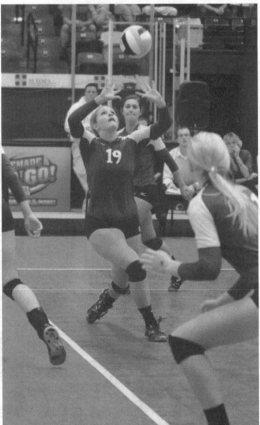

A state championship celebration.

Shelly Stumpff, Olivia Mekies, Olivia Fairfield, and Laynie Whitehead greet our fans after the match.

A group of us gathered at the bench in downtown Iowa City that was dedicated to Caroline and Ellyn.

L-R: Shelly Stumpff, Kelley Fliehler, Ernie Found, Olivia Mekies (Squeaks), Hannah Infelt, Scott Sanders and son Everett, and me.

Fun Sunday with Ernie, Frank Deford and Lisa Bennett the producer for HBO's Real Sports with Bryant Gumbel. Frank taking the time to read a letter I wrote him about Caroline and this incredible group of girls started us down the road that has led to this story now becoming a major motion picture. I think Line and Ellyn would think that is pretty neat. Unfortunately, Frank passed away in May 2017. I will always be grateful to him for helping us tell our story.

## CHAPTER 24

# CITY HIGH

It's sweltering in the City High School gymnasium here in Iowa City, even though it's the third week in September. The over-capacity crowd is going wild and the West High supporters are wearing their Live Like Line shirts. Students from both schools are taunting each other with cheers in support of their teams.

The West/City rivalry is second to none. The two schools often field the best athletes in the state, and tonight is no exception. The City High volleyball team is entering the match as the second-ranked large school in the state, and we are currently ranked third. Iowa City's bragging rights are at stake, and both teams want to claim the traveling trophy affectionately dubbed "The Spike"—this 16" tall trophy has a plain wood base and another wooden piece that sits perpendicular to the base. A bronze front attached to the upright piece has all the winning teams' names etched in since 1978. A gold painted railroad spike is glued prominently in the front of the trophy. The winner of the match gets to proudly display the award next to all the state championship ones in the trophy case and bragging rights are secured for the year. The City and West football teams play for the coveted "Boot" trophy— featuring a 1950's, gold-painted football cleat.

For me, the match doesn't carry the same importance now as it has in other years. For one thing, City High has supported us all season, standing by us the night of the visitation and even putting a tribute to Caroline on their team poster: a Spiderman in the upper right corner—Line's favorite superhero. The other reason is that I've gained new perspective; athletics is not life and death. Winning for the sake of winning isn't important to me anymore. My only concern is the fragile psyche of my players. A win over City doesn't carry the same importance that it used to.

I do hope for my girl's sake that they play well, because I know what this night means to them. This was Caroline's favorite match of the year because of the rivalry, and the girls desperately want to win for her and for themselves. Last year when City High beat us on our own court for the Spike, she furiously punched her locker—several of the girls thought she might have broken her hand. She had said then that there was no way City would beat us in her senior season.

But despite our 18-5 record, we played poorly in the Dubuque Wahlert tournament over the weekend, losing three of our six matches. In addition, we've barely practiced the past five days as the players struggled with their emotions. City High is loaded with talented hitters and their setter, Erin Muir, is an exceptional floor leader. This match will be a big challenge to see how well my girls keep their emotions in check and simply play volleyball.

The teams split the first two sets, 27-25 and 21-25. In the first set the West players were loose on the court, laughing and enjoying themselves. In the second set, it seemed like our nerves were getting the best of us. We missed too many serves and our defense was porous, our blockers weren't slowing down the City High hitters, and our serve reception was awful. Kelley was running all over the court trying to track down errant passes.

We switch courts and the girls gather around Scott and me. They look a little rattled. "We need to stay in the moment," I tell them. "Too many of you seem distracted by the crowd, your parents, and the television cameras. Keep your focus on the court and communicate better with your teammates."

Scott jumps in. "Blockers, commit to their outside hitters and let's not worry so much about their middles. We need to slow down their offense and control the net."

The girls run out to the court and I turn to Scott, "This next game might define the remainder of our season. The question is, can they control their emotions and how will they respond to adversity?"

He nods in agreement

The official blows the whistle to start play, and Kelley steps behind the line and serves a tough ball, but City has no problem handling it. Erin Muir receives a great pass and sends the ball to the far side of the court. City's outside hitter, Rachael Rinehart, takes a huge swing but Fairfield and Whitehead block the hit straight down to the floor. My two blockers turn away from the net smiling as the rest of the team members jump in the air and scream. From that moment on, we play with determination and confidence. Shelly and Olivia slam kill after kill, Laynie and Hannah shut down City's offense at the net, and Squeaks and Anna give Kelley perfect passes to run the offense. We dominate the next two sets with the scores 25-16 and 25-19.

When the final point hits the floor, some of my girls begin to cry as they walk to the net to shake hands with the City High players. Even though this win over the 2nd ranked team in the state shows we're a legitimate contender for a state title, I can tell by their faces that they aren't feeling the same happiness as they have in previous years when they won The Spike. Instead they look more relieved than anything.

The seniors run over to the score table and grab the insignificant looking trophy. They race to the top bleacher where Ernie has been standing and applauding. They reverently present him with the coveted award. With the girls hugging him from each side, Ernie triumphantly raises The Spike in the air as tears stream down his face.

I turn away from the scene and sit back down on the bench. I bury my head in my hands; it's too hard to watch the girls' and Ernie's raw emotion. This win is so hard to enjoy without Caroline here to share the excitement.

Jeff Linder, a reporter for the *Cedar Rapids Gazette*, sits down next to me. "I know this is tough, Brez. Can you say what this win means to you and your team?"

I consider Jeff a friend, but I can't give him the well-thought-out answer that he deserves. I'm not sure I can even talk. I finally look up at him and blurt out the only thing that's on my mind, "I miss my player."

He nods empathetically and pats my shoulder, then he gets up to talk to someone else.

Once I finally get control of my emotions, I stand up and accept congratulations from well-wishers. I make my way toward the exit and see Scott standing by the wall next to the door. I go over and we share a long hug.

Nothing about this season is easy.

# CHAPTER 25
# LIVE LIKE LINE: NURTURING

It's been three weeks since our big victory over City High. Since then, the girls seem to be getting physically and emotionally weaker. To an outsider it would seem that our team is on a magical journey. We lose our top player and yet we're 27-6, we've won two of three weekend tournaments and now, because top-ranked Ankeny lost coupled with our win over City High, we're the top-ranked 5A team in the state. However, an outsider can't see our unproductive practices every night, when the girls are either goofing around or crying. It's so frustrating. It's my responsibility as their coach to help them deal with their grief and to prepare them for the post-season. But I feel like I'm failing miserably, and I'm not sure I've put them in a position to succeed.

There are two specific areas of our game that I worry about: our mental state and our conditioning level. During matches we play just well enough to win. We're capable of competing with any of the top teams in the state, but I keep waiting for the roof to fall in. One big loss, like Senior Night or during the conference tournament, and the remainder of the season could head in a downward spiral. If I can't get West volleyball back to the state tournament, my girls will be devastated. I will have failed them.

Our lack of conditioning on the team haunts me. Most seasons we're able to train the girls for a two-hour, high-pressure match. But this season that's been impossible to accomplish. We've been successful at the long Saturday tournaments but those best-of-three matches aren't the same as a two-hour, best-of-five, high-pressure situation. I'm not sure we're physically capable of playing a full five-set match.

Stress is compromising the girls' immune systems, so many of them have missed practice because of severe colds or the flu. They're much too young to take on so much pressure. They have the pressure of being ranked number one as well their internal pressure to win for Line and the community, all on top of their own debilitating grief.

It's Friday. We're having another poor practice and I'm losing patience. I'm not angry at them, but I haven't had a complete night's rest since Caroline's accident, and the lack of sleep is starting to wear me down too.

I call the team over to me on the sideline. "Since we don't have a tournament tomorrow, why don't we call it a day? Do something away from the volleyball court. Head to the West High football game with your friends, have supper with your family, or just chill out."

Scott seems as shocked as the players. Usually I would consult with him before I cancelled practice, but I know I can't be in this gym for one more minute. The girls are excited by my announcement and quickly exit the gymnasium.

Scott turns to me and says, "Are you okay?"

"Yeah," I reply. "I think the girls need a break." I don't want to admit to him that I'm the one who needs a break—a break from volleyball, the kids, and the pressure.

I feel like my insides are going to burst as I walk into the locker room. I barely get inside my office when all my emotions come to the surface. I sit at my desk, and begin to sob. *I can't be strong anymore, I can't do this. This season is going to fall apart and it's going to be my fault. I'm going to fail these girls. I miss Line so much.*

"Line," I say through my tears. "I need to know you're okay. I need to know that you're still with us in some way. I know everyone is asking you to be there for them, but please give me some kind of sign. It doesn't have to be anything big, darn it, just something."

Of course nothing happens—no apparition appears hovering in front of me, no large clap of thunder sounds—just the silence of a locker room on a Friday night. I stay there for a few more minutes to compose myself, then I grab my briefcase to go home. I open my office door and am startled to see two West High students on the other side of the room getting jackets from their lockers. Embarrassed by my tear-reddened eyes, I can only hope they didn't hear my outburst or my sobbing in my office. I greet them as they leave, and then fumble with the key to lock the door. I glance down at the floor and see two pennies sitting on the threshold of my office. I know they weren't there when I went into the office a couple of minutes ago.

Could this be my sign from Caroline, I wonder? I've always heard that pennies found in groups of three are pennies from heaven. I notice both pennies are turned heads up when I bend down to grab them. If this is a sign, I need to find the third penny. I'm almost frantic as I search the floor and look under locker room benches, all to no avail. There isn't a third penny anywhere.

"Dang it, Caroline, quit messing with me!" I yell out loud. "I can't take anymore. Why do you always need to mess with me? Where is the other penny?"

My shout echoes back to me in the empty locker room and I belatedly hope the two students, who just left the room, didn't hear me. I'm being foolish, I know this isn't a sign from Caroline. I'm grasping at straws.

I slowly walk to the back entrance of the locker room, my feet heavy and my heart broken. I look down at the floor as I reach for the doorknob and there it is: the third penny, facing heads up. I clasp the three pennies in my fist and hold them to my heart. Somehow I know,

I feel it in my soul, that Caroline sent me this sign to say she was all right.

"Thanks, Line," I say. I walk to the car, my soul healed – at least for today.

## CHAPTER 26

# SCOTT SANDERS

"**O**h my God, I *hate* stadium cleanup."
With a grunt and a heave, I toss another
overflowing garbage bag into the compactor. The bag
must have a tear in the bottom because when I raise it
up, a disgustingly rancid combination of beer, pop, and
other unidentifiable fluids runs down my outstretched
arm and soaks my shirt. Scott begins to laugh and I
grab a hot dog bun from the food recycling bin. My
sidearm toss is right on target and the bun hits him on
the side of the head, the ketchup mixing with his short-
cropped sandy-brown hair and splattering his
dark-rimmed glasses. I run back into the building and
push in the button to summon the elevator.

We're here with about 700 other people to clean up
the University of Iowa's Kinnick Stadium after
yesterday's football game. Every Sunday morning after
the University of Iowa plays a home game, all the junior
high and high school athletes in the Iowa City school
district descend on the stadium at 7:30 in the morning
and pick up all the trash in the bleachers, luxury suites,
and food court. In return, the university donates a
substantial amount of money to the Iowa City schools'
athletic booster clubs. West High volleyball was lucky to
get the assignment of cleaning up the press box and
luxury suites a few years ago. It means we're inside the
building and don't have to deal with rainy fall weather or
even snow at the end of the season. I don't miss trying

to sweep up peanut shells and side-stepping the vomit and chewing tobacco that's often frozen onto the stadium cement floor.

Not that cleaning up the four stories of luxury suites is that wonderful. It's a surprisingly messy job cleaning these rooms, particularly the media area. We have to pick up hundreds of cups half-filled with leftover soda or coffee and dump the contents into a bucket. Copious amounts of paper – press guides, game programs, and newspapers – have to be recycled, as do all refundable cans and bottles. We have to empty all the trash cans, including the ones in the bathroom, then take all the garbage and recyclables down in the single elevator to the ground floor. We can usually finish in ninety minutes as long as most of our freshman, sophomore, and varsity volleyball players show up on time. Stadium cleanup is a win–win situation for both the University of Iowa and our athletic programs, but it's asking a lot of my varsity athletes to do this after they've participated in an eleven-hour Saturday tournament the day before. It really cuts into their study, family, and relaxation time.

I stand in the cement-block entrance waiting for the elevator to arrive, hoping it gets here before Scott catches up with me. I hear it creaking down from the fourth floor, agonizingly slow. I can see Scott charging around the corner of the recycling area with a tray of cheesy nachos covered with, I'm guessing, fly eggs. The elevator finally arrives and the doors open and I quickly enter and jab the close-door button just in time. I can hear Scott pounding on the doors as the elevator begins its slow ascent.

I get off the elevator, step into the first suite down the hall, and grab another bag of garbage. I'm startled less than two minutes later when I hear a footstep behind me and I turn around in time to see Scott rushing toward me with his right hand tucked behind his back. I bring my arms up protectively around my head. "No, don't!" I yell. I assume he still has that gelatinous mass of nacho chips and cheese cupped in his hand.

He doesn't say a word as he advances toward me. I stick out both arms and try to push him away, but he's much stronger than I am. He pins me against the counter and whips his right hand from behind his back and slaps it on top of my head. I wait to feel the goo ooze down my scalp but nothing happens—his hand is empty.

"Ha, I got you," he says smugly.

Relieved that my hair isn't covered with smashed chips and cheese sauce, I start to laugh and Scott joins in and pretty soon we're bending over, out of control, laughing our heads off. Several of our players nervously glance into the suite to see what's going on—generally there isn't a lot of laughing while we clean up garbage at 7:30 in the morning. Anna appears in the doorway, shakes her head and walks away. This makes us laugh even harder. Tears run down my face.

This is Scott's third season as my assistant and he's been a tremendous asset to our program. We've made it to the championship match of the state tournament for the past two years, and I attribute much of that success to him. He's the yin to my yang. Whereas I'm an offensive coach, he excels at teaching defense. I'm very emotional, yelling and pacing during games, and he's Mr. Steady Eddy. We make a great coaching combination, but I've come to appreciate his friendship even more than his coaching expertise.

I'm very independent and it's not easy for me to open up to others or ask for help, especially when it involves my personal life. Scott was just beginning his tenure with me in August of 2009 when I had to pull him aside and confide that my seventeen-year relationship was ending. I would be selling my house and looking for a new place to live. My life was in turmoil and I was an emotional wreck. I wanted him to be prepared in case I had to leave practice for one reason or another. I barely knew this man, but he reached out, took my hand, and told me that I was more than welcome to move in with him and Sheena, his soon-to-be fiancé. I looked at him, at his kind blue eyes behind his glasses, his short sandy hair, his sincere solemn expression, and I smiled and said how much I appreciated his offer. I didn't take him up on it though—I'd always kept a certain distance between me and my assistants and my players.

That distance disintegrated the day Caroline died, and now Scott's chasing me with imaginary nachos and, more than that, we're friends—true friends. He's become my confidante, my sounding board, the person who hugs and comforts me when I'm feeling wretched about the pain my girls are in. I've leaned on him for emotional support this season, not just during the days immediately following Caroline's death—the visitation and funeral—but during our everyday routines since then. Sometimes when I least expect it, the tiniest little thing triggers an overwhelming sense of loss in me. Scott, with his innate empathy, senses how I'm feeling and clasps me to him in a reassuring embrace. And more often than not, I see grief in his eyes too.

Scott is fairly quiet and reserved himself, nachos-chase notwithstanding, but as our friendship has grown over the last year he's opened up more to me too. We can, and have, talked about almost anything. And he's grown more confident as a coach over the last two years. He suggests line-up changes and strategic moves. I value his input and I almost always follow his suggestions.

What I enjoy most about Scott is his dry sense of humor. I never know what he might say during a tense time during a match, but somehow he always manages to lighten the mood. It might be making a funny comment about a volleyball official or giving me a hard time about being so much older than he is. His teasing never goes too far though, and his quick wit keeps the girls and me entertained.

"Hey, I'm thinking about having an optional practice when we get done here," Scott says when we finally finish laughing. "I haven't had one in a couple of weeks. Feel free to join us if you want."

"I think I'll pass," I say with a smile.

Scott has been holding what he calls "optional practices" on Sunday mornings after stadium cleanup. He's had two or three of them so far this season. Generally these occur when we haven't played a tournament the day before. I've never gone because I think it's a good opportunity for him to solidify his relationship with the players and assert his authority. It's not easy being an assistant coach, and this is a chance for him to be in charge of the team. It's a more relaxed atmosphere than our normal afternoon practices after school. Not everyone attends the optional practices, so he can give one-on-one instruction and gear the drills with individual improvement in mind rather than team-centered instruction.

We haul the final bags of garbage to the elevator, and on the ride down Scott tells the girls to join him at West High in thirty minutes if they want to do some optional ball-handling. I see Shelly and Squeaks look at each other and smile. This seems odd to me but I don't say anything because it's Scott's gig— I have no intention of walking into our gymnasium on a Sunday, my one day off.

I say good-bye to the girls and Scott and head to Aldi's to pick up a few staples for the week. During my drive to the store, I keep thinking about the look that passed between Shelly and Squeaks. What was that about? Any time I've asked them how one of Scott's optional practices went, they've been evasive. Either they casually say something like "Oh it was fine," or if there's more than one player present, they all start chuckling.

Standing in the produce section trying unsuccessfully to pick out the perfect cantaloupe, I make a tentative decision: I should go over to West High next. If I don't see what's going on in these practices of Scott's, it's going to bug me all day.

I pay for my purchases, walk out to the car, and toss the bags in the back of my black Honda Insight. I'm still indecisive about whether I should go to the practice. I don't want Scott to think I'm intruding. But when I get to the parking lot exit, I turn on my left directional signal and head in the opposite direction from my house.

I get to West High and pull into one of the parking spots reserved for custodians. Only one janitor will be working on a Sunday, and if I park here it's unlikely any of the girls or Scott will see my car. I quietly unlock the door near the boys' locker room and gently ease the door shut behind me. Walking up the back steps to the gym balcony, I hear laughter rising above Bruno Mars "Just the Way You Are." The music must be coming from our portable speaker system.

I reach the top step and see with dismay that the curtain used to close off the balcony from the gym below is pulled back. Almost the entire expanse of the upper deck is visible from the courts. I only have a three-foot area to stand in where I'm not visible to Scott or the girls. I wedge myself between the wall and the bunched up curtain and peek through the narrow four-inch gap. Down below most of the girls are grouped together laughing and pointing at something or someone in the direction of the net. I have to pull the curtain back a bit to see the source of their amusement.

*What the heck?*

Squeaks is balanced precariously on Shelly's shoulders while at the same time holding onto one of the volleyball standards – the poles that hold up the net – with one hand. Shelly is either struggling with balancing 110 pounds on her shoulders or she's intentionally trying to scare Squeaks, because she's staggering around beside the net. Her legs appear to buckle under Squeak's squirming weight and Squeaks screams. The rest of the girls are clearly enjoying the spectacle, particularly Kelley. She's doubled over with laughter, her hands on her knees.

Squeaks reaches up as high as she can, straining to hang a bright pink bra from the top of the net antenna, which is nine feet above the floor of the court. She completes her mission, then wraps both arms around the pole and half jumps, half climbs, off Shelly's shoulders to the safety of the court. The rest of the girls whoop and applaud.

I'm fit to be tied. Both of them could have been seriously hurt. And the big question I have is where's Scott during this debacle? I'm furious. It's one thing to lose a starter to an injury that might occur while playing volleyball, but it's an entirely different matter if you lose a starter because they were screwing around while unsupervised.

"Butterfly passing," I hear Scott yell. He's coming into the gym pushing two carts full of volleyballs. The girls immediately sober up and act as if nothing untoward has happened. They jog over to him and grab ten volleyballs. They begin the serving and passing drill and Scott moves near the center of the court. He looks up at an errant pass and I can see the shocked look on his face when he notices the pink bra.

"Oh my God, who did that?" he bellows.

The girls all look over at Squeaks and she tentatively raises her hand.

"Get that off there. *Now.* This is how coaches get fired!"

Squeaks quickly runs over to the volleyball pole and jumps into the air in an attempt to reach the bottom of the dangling pink bra. She misses several times and Scott's face gets redder and redder. When Squeak's hand gets tangled in the net on her fourth attempt, the rest of the girls drop to their knees on the court with laughter. Finally Shelly joins Squeaks and lifts her into the air. Squeaks successfully grabs the bra, Shelly lets go of her legs, and Squeaks hurriedly stuffs the bra into her duffel bag, sitting a few feet away. Scott shakes his head with disgust. It's apparent that he's lost all semblance of order during this Sunday's practice.

I've seen enough. Easing away from the gap between the curtain and the wall so that no one notices me, I slip down the back staircase and out the door. I don't even make it to my car before I burst out laughing. Despite my initial reaction, the entire scene I just watched was pretty funny. Scott probably doesn't realize it, but his optional practices may be the most important ones of the year. The girls need this kind of emotional outlet. I don't know what I'd do without him.

## CHAPTER 27

# CAN WE HANDLE PRESSURE?

**C**oaches worry.

It's the nature of the beast. Even under the best of circumstances everything worries me during the season. I worry about developing my players. I worry about them playing to their potential. I worry about getting the travel details right. It's how I roll. This season I'm worrying even more than ever before.

It's Thursday, October 13th, and we have the most important tournament of the season this Saturday – our conference tournament. Six out of the fourteen teams playing are ranked in the top ten, including City High, ranked second. We've won our conference tournament three years in a row. I'm sure we're considered a favorite to win it again this season, but I don't share those sentiments.

We haven't played well since we beat City High a month ago. We're still playing just well enough to beat average teams, but we don't look sharp. This past weekend we made it to the championship match in the Westside tournament in Cedar Rapids – one of the premier tournaments in the state – but then we lost the match, to Tripoli, the top-ranked 1A school. Tripoli has a great volleyball program and there isn't any embarrassment in losing to them, but right now I don't feel as if we're ready to compete in the post-season, which is coming up in two weeks.

I don't have my team prepared—mentally or

physically—to make a run for a state title. I tossed and turned all through the night, chastising myself for doing a crappy job as their coach. The only thing that matters to these girls is winning a state championship for Caroline, and I haven't put them in a position to be successful. If I don't start demanding more from my players during practice, I will have failed them and I'll never forgive myself.

Practice today is going the same as every day. My players aren't communicating, they're letting balls drop to the floor untouched, and they look like they want to be anywhere but in this gym. Hannah, in particular, acts as if she's working a nine-to-five job instead of playing a sport she loves. She's sullen and despondent. When her teammates try to cheer her up, she brushes them off.

Something has to change and it has to change now.

"Everyone on the endline," I yell.

If the girls are surprised, their faces don't show it. They jog over to the side of the court and look at me expectantly. I'm not even sure what I'm going to have them do—this wasn't in my practice plans.

I toss a volleyball to Shelly. "Shell, serve to zone six. If you miss the serve *everyone* has to do two ladders." Ladders are a running drill that involves running three different distances back and forth across the gym. They're physically taxing—they use up all the energy reserves stored in the muscles of whoever is doing them. My players hate ladders. In most seasons we do them at least once a week in practice. We haven't done them at all so far this season because I've been afraid they couldn't handle the additional stress.

"If you serve to the wrong zone," I reiterate to Shelly, "everybody will do two ladders. If you serve zone six, practice is over." Servers have to be able to serve to the zone on the court that their coach wants them to—Scott's responsible for signaling our serves. Zone one is the deep right back of the court. Zone six is the center of the back of the court; it's the easiest zone to serve to.

I've picked Shelly for this exercise for two reasons. One, because she jump-serves. Jump-serving is difficult to do. The server backs up ten feet behind the endline and tosses the ball high in the air in front of her. Then she leaps into the air and hits the ball. When successfully accomplished, a jump-serve is a thing of beauty. The ball has a great deal of topspin that causes it to drop with a tremendous velocity, making it difficult to successfully pass. She's leading our team in ace serves—serves that score a point because the other team can't return the ball.

The second reason I've picked her is that she's emerged as one of the most consistent leaders on the team this season. She's the one person most likely to pat the back of a struggling teammate or yell encouragement to her teammates when we're struggling. My hope is that she can make this serve to not only end practice, but to demonstrate that she can perform under pressure, both to me and her teammates.

Coaches have different philosophies regarding serving. Some coaches want their players to do tough serves every time, trying to score points off ace serves all the time, which is a high-risk/high-reward philosophy. Personally, I would like my players to go for easier serves to increase the odds of a higher serving percentage, rather than risk having them miss a serve and give the other team an automatic point. I want to make our opponents earn their points instead of handing it to them with service errors. Because we're not serving tough, we have to be able to consistently put the ball where we want it to go with our serves. This allows us to exploit our opponent's weakness.

Shelly slowly walks to the endline as her teammates watch. She tosses the ball into the air and makes good contact. Her serve goes over the net but goes to the wrong side of the court, to zone 1 instead of zone 6. Without me saying a word, she and her teammates begin to run ladders. They run thirty feet, touch the line, and then return to their starting spot. They turn around without stopping and run sixty feet, touch that line, and return again to the starting spot. Then they run the full length of the court and back. Then, without stopping, they have do another whole set of sprints across the gym—another ladder—all because of Shelly's miscue.

They finish the two ladders and bend over with their hands on their knees to catch their collective breath. I look around for another senior to be the server in this exercise—we won't stop until someone serves to the correct zone. The longer it takes to get it right, the more difficult it will become, because whoever's serving will have to deal with being exhausted as well as the pressure of making the serve.

"Squeaks, zone two, for three ladders," I say.

Squeaks sometimes struggled during the previous season when she had to perform under pressure. When she got ace served or failed to dig up a tipped ball, she would respond by grabbing her hair—as if to pull it out—and dropping her head toward the floor. Caroline was constantly trying to reassure her, and I was constantly subbing her out of the game for letting our opponents see her negative reactions. Now I watch her carefully select a volleyball from the cart and walk to the endline. I believe that she'll put this serve in the correct zone. She's playing with so much more confidence this season, talking on the court, and controlling her body language. She turns her hips to the intended zone and tosses the ball in the air. Her floater serve lands four feet beyond the endline of the court.

With an audible groan, the girls begin to run the three-ladder consequence for the missed serve. I look over at Scott and he shrugs as if to say, "If they can't make the serves in practice, they won't make them when it matters."

For the next five minutes I watch player after player

fail the serving assignment. My girls are beyond the point of exhaustion. Whenever I've done something like this before, the drill ended with the third or fourth attempt. My heart goes out to them. I want to end practice and send them home, but I know I can't. They have to be able to handle extreme pressure. I also don't want them to go home feeling like failures. They need to accomplish this goal today.

It comes to me what I should do. "Hannah, serve the ball anywhere on the court and practice is over. If you miss, we have ten ladders." Ten ladders is an absurd number, but I know there's no chance one of my varsity athletes can't put a ball over the net and land it somewhere on the opposite court.

Hannah takes her place behind the serving line and pushes her sweat-drenched blonde hair away from her face. We all watch her draw a big breath, gently toss the ball in the air, and make contact. The wobbly serve doesn't even make it to the net. Hannah drops to the floor, puts her head on her arms, and begins sobbing uncontrollably. Her teammates, frustrated, once again begin to run.

I walk over to Hannah, but before I can say an encouraging or consoling word to her, she jumps up and joins her teammates sprinting down the court, tears pouring from her eyes. I feel like such a hard-ass. I want to tell them to stop running, but I know I can't. I'm responsible for preparing them to step up and perform the way they've been trained to, when everything is at stake.

After only three ladders I tell them to stop running. "Hannah, serve," I say. "Serve the ball anywhere on the court and we're done. If you miss, we have fifteen ladders and this time we will run all of them."

I have to give her the opportunity to redeem herself, to succeed. I don't even realize I'm holding my breath until I see her make the serve and exhale with relief. The rest of the girls shout and clap her on the back. *Finally.* I can end practice on a high note. I look at Hannah. I expect to see her smiling, but instead I see her grimacing, still on the verge of tears.

I put my arm around her shoulder as the two of us make our way toward the gymnasium door. "Way to come through when it matters," I say and give her a gentle hug.

"It wasn't good enough," she says grimly. "I should have made the first one." She turns her back to me at the locker room door.

"Hannah. You'll come through for your teammates when it matters," I say to her.

She doesn't turn around. She simply nods and continues walking.

Later that evening I send Scott a text. "No practice tomorrow. It's time for a come-to-Jesus meeting." He sends me back a smiley face. I want to meet with the girls off the court and have a frank discussion. I need to figure out where their heads are. The conference tournament is on Saturday and our post-season play starts at the end of next week. We're clearly not ready.

Now it's 3:30 the next day. Friday afternoon. I watch my players slowly trudge into my classroom and drop down into the student desks I've pulled into a semicircle facing the front of the room. It's pretty unorthodox to cancel practice the day before the biggest tournament of the regular season, and I'm probably the only coach in the state who would do that. My girls are physically capable of playing well—but they need help with the head part of the game. These are intelligent young women and they know something's up if we're in a classroom instead of on the court. Instead of joking around, they're sitting somberly in their seats, whispering to one another.

I wait for Anna to arrive. She's always late. A couple of weeks ago, Jackie Green, Anna's first period teacher, approached me at lunch and said that Anna was late to class almost every day. This type of behavior is totally unacceptable to me. I expect my girls to set a good example both on and off the court. This tardiness is similar to some of Line's behaviors that would annoy me, such as disrupting a class with her incessant socializing. Unchecked, small things can result in a team being undisciplined and unfocused—a recipe for failure. I assured Jackie that I would talk to Anna and that it wouldn't happen again. At the start of practice that day, I pulled her aside and told her I was disappointed about her tardiness, that it reflected poorly on her and her teammates. Always quiet and not one to argue or make excuses, she sheepishly smiled and admitted that she was late too often and readily agreed to get to school on time from that point forward.

I thought the matter was taken care of until Jackie approached me in the hall three days later with the news that Anna was late for class again. That afternoon my players had just finished their warm-ups and were set to ball handle when I told them all to line up on the side line of the court. "*Ladders,*" I barked. "Everyone except Anna."

Several of the girls quickly glanced over at her and Anna's face turned ashen. It only took her seconds before she realized that her teammates were running because of her tardiness that morning.

"No, Brez, no. Don't make them run for my mistake... please. Let me run instead of them," she said.

I ignored her pleading and told the girls to run another ladder. I needed Anna and the others to understand that we were all accountable for each other. She anchors our defense as our primary passer. If she couldn't take care of a simple thing like getting to school on time, how could we depend on her during a match? Anna leaned forlornly against the pushed in bleachers and watched her teammates run. When they were done, she walked up to them to apologize and explain what happened. I could see several of them muttering under their breath to each other as they walked out for water.

I'm sure I was the target of their anger, but they needed to understand that our success during the remainder of this season depends on how well they stick together and how well they put the team ahead of themselves.

Today, I glare at Anna as she hurries into the room and she mouths the word "Sorry." She quickly finds an empty seat and Scott firmly shuts the door. The girls' last-ditch hope that we might watch game film vanishes when I hand each of them a piece of paper and a pencil. I move to the front of the room, pause and look around the circle. I look at each girl before moving on to the next. Some of them are looking up, but most of them are nervously playing with their pencils or doodling on the paper. This season I've tried to keep things light to try to take their minds off Caroline, and I can see they're not comfortable now that I'm getting serious.

"We need to talk. To most outside observers, we are having an amazing season. We're the top-ranked team in the state, we've won two tournaments and we're favored to win our fourth consecutive conference tournament championship tomorrow. But I know better. I feel like you're all holding back, that you're refusing to be great. I need to know what's going on—what are you feeling?"

I stop talking and wait for someone to answer my question. No one says a word. No one—except a couple of junior varsity athletes—will even look me in the eyes. I wait patiently for several minutes, but am met with silence.

Their reaction doesn't surprise me. In fact, I half expected it. They are so emotionally vulnerable that it's easy for them to put walls up to guard their feelings.

"Okay, we'll go about this another way. You have five minutes to write your answer to this question."

I turn around and write on the white board: "Why are you afraid of being good?"

A few of the girls begin immediately to write, while most of the others seem lost in thought. This exercise could backfire on me. I know it could bring their grief to the forefront and upset them or make them angry. But right now, I'm not sure how to move forward for the remainder of the season from a coaching standpoint without trying something like this.

The quiet of the room is suddenly broken by my classroom door being thrown open. Lexi Potter, our all-state middle blocker from the previous season, bursts in the room and says, "Oh my God, I've missed you guys and wanted to be with you so badly." Lexi plays volleyball for Wingate University in North Carolina now and was the only graduate from last year's team who wasn't able to come back for Caroline's visitation. She begins to cry as my players surround her and start giving her hugs.

I walk over and embrace her. I know she felt isolated and that no one on her college volleyball team could really understand what she was going through. "Welcome home," I say.

She smiles as tears run down her cheeks. At that moment it hits me, Line's tragic death really has made us all a family. My slight irritation about having my meeting interrupted evaporates. What we were going to do before Lexi showed up doesn't matter. One of our own has come home to grieve with her sisters. I know my "coming to Jesus" talk has ended before it even started and that's okay. Today Lexi needed us and that was more important than anything I had planned.

## CHAPTER 28
# MVC TOURNAMENT

"**D**ang it, Squeaks, don't hang your head when you make a mistake. *Next ball*," I scream with frustration. She's resorting back to the negative behaviors that she used to do.

We're playing Waterloo West in morning pool play of the Mississippi Valley Conference volleyball tournament. The tournament is hosted by a different school every year, and this is our year to host. We're not looking sharp even though we're playing on our home court. It's our opening match and we've already dropped the first set to Waterloo 14 - 21. They're a scrappy team but unranked, and have not had the same quality program we've had for the past four years. I can't believe we've started the tournament this way.

All week I had a sense of foreboding: this was going to be the weekend that we collapsed. Many coaches try to downplay the strength of their team, especially when they're favored to win, but I don't normally do that. If I think we're good enough to win, I'm going to say exactly that whether it's to the media or to my players. But not today. Today feels different. I truly don't feel we'll win this tournament and the way we're playing against Waterloo West right now only adds to my conviction. It's not that I care so much about the winning, but rather that I'm worried about how my girls will react if we end up having a terrible day. We're at the end of the regular season and if we're going to have a shot at getting to the state tournament, now is when we need to start playing our best volleyball.

Laynie Whitehead, our ninth grader, commits her second consecutive hitting error, one going into the net and this one out-of-bounds. I get the official's attention and request a time-out.

The girls jog slowly over to Scott and me at the bench. I tell Scott to talk to the team and I pull Kelley to the side, away from the others. "What's going on out there? Why would you set Laynie another ball when she just committed a hitting error?"

"I don't know," Kelley answers in a quiet voice. Then she says, "Laynie's hitting against their shortest blocker and I wanted to give her some confidence."

Her answer makes me pause. Her rationale is exactly right. Laynie does have the shortest player trying to block her and we can't just depend on Shelly and Eunice to put the hits down. We need a more balanced attack. Kelley is starting to think like a setter on the court. I need to trust her judgment. I know I need to reassure her—help her feel confident about her decision-making. "You're absolutely right, Kell. Balance out our attack with different hitters, but when we need a big point, set either Shelly or Eunice."

She nods and joins her teammates for a quick drink of water.

The very first play after our timeout, Kelley receives a perfect pass from Anna and she backsets the ball to Laynie, even though Eunice was approaching for a quick attack.

"Oh no," I mutter under my breath. What's Kelley thinking? This time, however, our lanky, left-handed freshman comes through with a dynamic hit that goes straight to the floor. No Waterloo player has a chance to get a hand on the ball.

Laynie smiles as the rest of the players crowd around to congratulate her. Kelley looks over to the bench and I give her a wink. I need to trust my setter more. She's doing a great job running the team, even with only two months of training. If she becomes confident and comfortable in the setting role, we'll be a much better team.

Laynie's kill seems to give us some fire and we play better than we have. Hannah and Olivia get some key blocks and we win the second set 21 – 13. The third and deciding set, we completely dominate Waterloo West and win 15 - 4. It wasn't a perfect start to the day, but we got the win.

We're off for a match so the girls go to the team room to eat some of the food their parents have brought them: bagels, sandwiches, fruit, and other snacks. I turn around from the scoring table, and Kelley's walking towards me with her mom, dad, and three people I've never seen before. The man and woman are in their late forties and wearing bright neon-green t-shirts that read "I ♥ Kelley." Kelley's talking excitedly to the third visitor, a girl about her age who's also sporting a Kelley t-shirt.

"Brez, I'd like you to meet my Uncle Bob and Aunt Donna and my cousin Abby. They drove up from Indiana this weekend to watch us play," Kelley says.

"Very nice to meet you three. I can't believe *anyone* would drive that far just to watch Kelley play," I say with a smile.

I extend my hand to Kelley's uncle but he ignores my offer of a handshake and pulls me to him in an embrace.

"Thanks for taking care of our niece," he whispers in my ear. "She's very special to us."

I take a half-step back so that I can look up at him. "She's pretty special to me as well." In order to lighten the mood I continue, "Hey, I would love one of those neon Kelley shirts. I would wear it to school *every day*."

"Eww," Kelley grimaces. "That's just too creepy."

We talk for a bit more and I watch Kelley laughing and talking with her cousin. I love seeing her so happy and acting like a regular teenage girl.

If I was hoping we'd play stronger after our hour

break, I hoped wrong. We struggle to beat Cedar Rapids Xavier 21 – 17 and 21 -14, and we drop the second set against Cedar Rapids Washington 18 – 21 after easily beating them 21 – 12 in the first.

As my girls huddle together on the court to start the third and deciding set with Washington, Scott nudges me with his elbow and motions with his head to the endline of the court. I see all the City High players sitting along the gym wall. I'm sure Craig Pitcher, their coach, has told them to watch our game and possibly pick up some of our weaknesses in case we end up playing each other in the championship match. The City High girls have been dominating their opponents all day and they look rested and relaxed as they laugh and mess around with each other. They look like they're brimming with confidence and probably feel indestructible, especially considering the way we've been playing.

"Do you think they're laughing at us?" Scott asks.

"Probably not," I respond. "But I can't say I'd blame them if they were. We look terrible today. I'm sure City thinks our win against them a month ago was a fluke."

"Naw, quit worrying so much. It is what it is," Scott says. "There's no way Wash beats us in this set. Our girls will find a way to win. If we meet up with City later today, we'll find a way to win that one as well."

Scott's an eternal optimist. I hope he's right. If we can beat Washington in this match, we'll be in first place in our pool and have a much higher seeding when we move into championship play. City High, because they haven't dropped a game the entire day, have already secured the top seed. If we win this match, we'll be the second or third seed and that would mean that we won't play City until the championship match. I don't want to face them any sooner than we have to.

My players know what this match means as far as our seeding. They've played hundreds of high school and club tournaments throughout their careers and have a high volleyball IQ. I don't need to add to their pressure by saying anything. The deciding set—only a 15-point game—begins, and neither team establishes any early momentum. My girls don't look panicked on the court, but we're also not playing with a sense of urgency. But with the score tied at six, I finally see the spark I was looking for. Hannah, Eunice, and Laynie begin to control the net with impressive blocking which seems to energize the rest of our team. At the same time the Washington players become quieter. Their hitters are having a difficult time getting any hits past our front row and we go on a 7 – 0 run to pull away with a 15 – 8 victory. We've won our pool, but we've only played well in short spurts. There's no way we looked like the top-ranked 5A team in the state, and my players are as aware of that as I am.

We shake hands with the Washington players and staff, and I call the girls to follow me to the far side of the gym. The brackets for the championship part of the tournament are hanging on the wall and we watch, along with fifty other coaches and players, as Marv Reiland begins to write in the pairings for the championship bracket. City High went 6 – 0 in pool play and he writes their name down as the top seed. Dubuque Wahlert was 6 – 1 and they're the second seed. Our 6 – 2 pool record was just good enough for the third seed. I let out a deep breath – at least we won't have to play City High right away. I'm satisfied that we have as high a seed as we do.

The girls jog off to warm up while Scott and I wait for Marv to write in our opponent, the #6 seed. I groan silently when I see its Dubuque Hempstead, the fourth-ranked team in the state.

"Whew," Scott says. "This isn't going to be easy. If we beat Hempstead then we have to play Wahlert to get to the championship."

Dubuque Wahlert is still the top-ranked 4A team in the state, one enrollment size below us. We barely beat them in the championship match of the Caroline Found Extravaganza, the early season tournament that we hosted.

I know Scott's just making conversation but I'm not in the mood for small talk, I'm feeling anxious and just a little irritable. "Yeah, welcome to life in the Mississippi Valley Conference," I say with a small tight smile.

Scott puts his arm over my shoulders as we walk across the gym to join the girls. "Relax. They're going to start playing better. I think we're going to win this tournament."

"I don't know. City looks pretty unbeatable today. But I think we better worry about what we're going to do to beat the Hempstead Mustangs first. It would certainly suck to get beat out in the quarterfinals and have to sit around for the next three hours until the tournament gets over."

Because we're hosting the tournament, we have to stay until the end of the day to put the nets, standards, and equipment away. It'd be a lot more fun to be playing than to be eliminated early and have to watch the rest of the teams' battle it out for the championship.

# CHAPTER 29

# AN MVC CHAMPIONSHIP

The officials call for the captains of our two teams to meet near the scoring table. The referee goes over the ground rules and flips a coin to determine which team will serve first. Hempstead wins the flip and elects to receive serve. Now that we're out of pool play, the games will go to 25 points. The matches are still the best of three. When teams play a single match during the week the contests are always the best of five, but that wouldn't work for weekend tournaments – the tournaments would go on forever.

I give the girls a few basic instructions and they jog out onto the court. I watch them huddle together. I look at their expressions and body language to see how they're feeling going into this match, but I can't tell anything.

Kelley steps behind the endline and watches the official for the signal to serve. He motions with his arm toward the net and blows his whistle. Kelley contacts the ball and sends a perfect floater between two Hempstead players. It drops for a point. An ace serve. The rest of the players on our court rush back to Kelley, throw one hand out, their arms like spokes in a circle, and yell, "Ace!" This is what they always do when someone scores on a serve. Kelley's relatives, wearing their bright lime-green shirts, cheer wildly in the bleachers behind us and she tosses them a quick smile.

I lean back in my chair. It's only one point, but I

already feel better than I did fifteen minutes earlier. My girls seem more relaxed and confident too.

Kelley serves her second ball and my front-court blockers – Laynie, Hannah, and Shelly – look imposing as they stand at the net in pre-blocking stances. They appear determined to stop every Hempstead hit. The Hempstead setter sends the ball to their all-state hitter, Audrey Reeg, on the outside of the court. Laynie and Hannah time their block perfectly and stuff the ball back to Hempstead's side of the court. Anna jumps into the air, raising her feet to her butt, and lets out a loud scream of jubilation.

Scott turns to me. "I don't want to say I told you so, but I told you so. When the pressure's on, we're a different team."

"You're pretty smug," I say, smiling. "Especially for someone sitting in the second chair." Scott always refers to our positions as first and second chair.

"Yeah, well, I have to earn my salary," he says.

As the match continues it's apparent that today we're a better team than Hempstead. We win this quarterfinal match 25 -14 and 25 – 17.

City High easily defeated 11th-ranked Cedar Falls and they're already warming up for their semifinal match against Cedar Rapids Kennedy, the 7th-ranked team in the state. Kennedy has an experienced, senior-laden team, but I don't have any doubts that City will prevail. But, I can't worry about those two teams. My job is to get my girls focused on playing Wahlert for our semifinal matchup.

The officials for our match meet with the captains and each team is given three minutes to warm up on the court. Scott runs the girls through a few hitting drills and then brings them over to the sideline by our bench. The girls grab their water bottles from under the bench and join Scott and me. They put their arms around each other's waists and form a small, tight circle. If I thought my players would be energetic and vocal before our next match, with Wahlert, I was mistaken. They stand quietly as we huddle together before taking the court, their demeanor unchanged. My players listen intently to my instructions, but they look like they're ready to start an eight-hour work shift at a local convenience store. We're missing that one person to fire up everyone with passion and excitement:  we're missing Caroline Found.

The first set begins and the Wahlert players seem a little hesitant on the court. It could be because Anna and Squeaks are digging up every hit attempt or because Kelley is doing a great job getting the sets to Shelly and Eunice and they're putting down powerful kills. We execute well—offensively and defensively—and we hand the Golden Eagles a 25 – 17 loss.

"Great job," I say to my players before the start of the second set. "Let's continue to control the net and minimize our mistakes. We have the momentum. Don't let them back in the match. Dominate the first few points and we'll take this in two. *Let's go West.*" I muster as much enthusiasm as I can find in myself in an effort to get them excited. My girls got excited after winning big points during this first set, but their intensity level seems to be ebbing and flowing, which can be a recipe for disaster in a game in which momentum counts as much as talent.

"West on nine!" Shelly yells to her teammates.

The girls count to nine enthusiastically and run out onto the court and I smile. *Finally* they're acting as if they're ready to dominate an opponent.

My hope that we'll control the start of the second set and take Wahlert out of the game doesn't materialize. Our two teams trade points back and forth and when the Golden Eagles take an 11 – 9 lead, I can sense momentum beginning to shift to their side of the court. Now we're the ones missing serves, hitting balls out of bounds, and playing poorly, and the Wahlert players begin to feed off our mistakes. Their play improves tremendously compared to the first set, and they pull away with a convincing 25 – 19 win.

As the Wahlert girls leap with excitement on the final point, I turn to Scott. "This isn't what we needed." I only have three minutes to turn in the lineup card for the third set. I consider moving our lineup three rotations so that Shelly and Eunice both start in the front row, but decide not to make any changes and write Kelley's number in the first serving position.

"This is as good a time as any to see what we're made of," he says. "Do we have the resolve and determination to be a championship team?"

"Well, the girls seem to have the ability to step up their game based on the competition and the situation. Let's hope they can do that now."

The City High girls have already beaten Kennedy. They sit against the wall to watch our next game, exuding confidence. Their laughter fills the gym. They're enjoying the moment and they should. They've made it through the day without dropping a single set against some of the best teams in the state. They feel indestructible – as only seventeen-year-old athletes are capable of feeling.

Our deciding set against Wahlert begins like a ping pong match. Neither team can get more than a one-point lead.

Wahlert is leading 6 – 5, but then the chemistry of the match changes. Mollie Mason, our sophomore outside hitter who plays opposite Shelly, puts a nice touch shot down the line to tie the game. Shelly goes back and serves. The Wahlert girl can't control Shelly's difficult jump serve and the ball flies over the net, back to our side of the court—this is called a free ball. A free ball is an easy ball for our defenders to pass, and all three of our front court players quickly approach the net. It's going to be a low, fast set. A good team can convert free ball opportunities about eighty percent of the time for a point.

Shelly passes the free ball to the top of the net in front

of Kelley. Kelley rises into the air, and with Eunice and Laynie approaching the net on each side of her, delivers a beautiful quick set. Eunice times her jump perfectly and the Wahlert players don't have a chance of blocking or digging her hit. My girls execute the play to perfection.

This two-point run is all we need. Wahlert is unable to stop us for the next five points and we take an insurmountable 12 – 6 lead. Wahlert manages to score a couple of points but it isn't enough. We close out the match with a 15 – 8 win.

Our two teams shake hands. Wahlert coach Jan Tyne and I embrace when we get to the end of the receiving line. We wish each other good luck in the postseason and I turn my focus to the final match of the day. Both teams have already been in this gymnasium for over ten hours. City's gone a perfect 10 – 0, while we've had to play three more games than they have to make it this far. I worry that fatigue is going to be a factor once we step onto the court. Does my team have any energy reserves to tap into? I'm beginning to realize that I can't underestimate my players; they're playing for something much more important than a conference tournament championship. They're much more resolute than I've been giving them credit for.

The three-minute warm-up period ends and my girls circle around me. For the first time today, in fact for the first time in many weeks, I see something different in their eyes: steely determination. They're focused and confident. They stand before me with their shoulders back, not slumping the way they've been doing all day, and their heads held high.

I talk to them about focusing on the moment and not the end result. I remind them that controlling the net will have a great impact on which team wins this championship match. Eunice interrupts me. She turns to her teammates, looking almost angry. "Now's the time to step it up. We're not going to let a single ball touch the floor! *Let's do this, West,*" she yells.

The girls count to nine and run out onto the court. Scott puts Line's shoes under the first seat of our bench and we both sit down.

"How you feeling about this?" he asks.

I hesitate for just a moment. "An hour ago I would have said not a chance, but now I'm not sure. I haven't seen them look like this all season. Almost cocky. I like this change in them."

He elbows me gently in the ribs and gives me an impish grin. "Yep. Just remember it was the second chair who told you earlier that we were going to win this tournament."

The first set begins. The City High girls are loud and vocal when they score a point, but my players don't seem to even notice City's exuberance. Sometimes athletes get in a zone where they're so focused on their task they block out all external distractions. That's what appears to be happening to my players now.

The City High girls seem perplexed that they can't establish any momentum against a team that looked so mediocre all day. Clinging to a 13 – 11 lead, Shelly converts on a free ball opportunity, taking a giant swing on a fast set that Kelley shot to the outside of the court. Her floor-rattling kill could be a highlight on ESPN's SportsCenter. My players spontaneously jump into the air and scream. The rout is on. Eunice begins to shut down the City High hitters and we score seven unanswered points—four of those coming from blocks. City High doesn't respond when we toss down the gauntlet and we win the first set 25 – 14.

We drop the first two points of the second set, but tie the game with an ace serve by Squeaks and a kill from Laynie, both unlikely heroes. We rattle off three more points and I can sense the momentum shifting to our side of the court. The City hitters become frustrated with their inability to get the ball past our front row players. When Hannah scores two consecutive points with solo blocks, I stop pacing and coaching from the sideline of the court and walk down to the end of the bench and sit by Scott. I want to enjoy the rest of this match next to my friend.

Eunice extols her teammates to keep pushing. With her primal screams after every big point and her hitting and blocking prowess, it's almost as if she's determined to put this team on her shoulders and carry them to victory.

The rest of my players follow her lead and get more excited with each point we score. Shelly slams a free ball back across the net and we win the second set and the championship 25 -18. Our bench players race out to the floor and all the girls scream and jump around. Scott and I turn to each other and embrace without saying a word. I wipe the moisture from my eyes. We join the players on the floor and we all shake hands by the net.

"Congrats, Brez," Craig Pitcher says to me. "Your girls sure deserved to win this match."

I can see he's shocked by the loss. A few minutes later, when we're being interviewed by reporters, he tells Susan Harmon, who writes for the *Iowa City Press Citizen*, "They [West] found like four more gears after the Wahlert match. I think they want to beat us, as of right now, more than we want to beat them."

If I had heard him saying that I would have agreed with him. We played on autopilot the entire day and somehow the girls did find four more gears in that final match to dominate a seemingly unbeatable City High squad.

We gather together for pictures in front of the net. Squeaks and the Russian hold Caroline's #9 jersey in the front row, and the rest of us raise our medals and hold up four fingers to the camera—indicating the number of consecutive years we've won this tournament. Despite having been in this muggy gymnasium for more than eleven hours, playing volleyball for most of it, the girls are giddy. They mug for their parents' cameras. By now, everyone else has left and it's only us and them.

I'm glad they're feeling so energetic. We still have another half hour here putting all the nets and equipment away.

## CHAPTER 30

# SENIOR NIGHT

Tonight is Senior Night, the night we honor our senior players, three days after the MVC tournament. It's a beautiful fall evening and we're playing our final home match of the regular season. Scott and I stand in the doorway of the gym, watching students, parents, and fans fill the bleachers to capacity. I know my girls have finished their dancing ritual and are waiting for us to join them in the team room. Honoring the seniors and their parents before this match is always a way to thank them for all their hard work and dedication. But this year Senior Night feels different; I've been dreading this night for weeks.

"Scott, I don't know if I can walk into that team room and face those girls," I say. "Every girl in that room remembers this is the match that Caroline talked about all summer. She wanted her mom to be with her for Senior Night."

"We can't wait much longer," Scott replies. "Let's get it over with."

We turn away from the gym entrance and walk back to the team room. Normally before a match, music would be blaring and the girls would be jumping around in anticipation, but tonight there's silence as Scott and I enter the room. As I talk about our game plan for Dubuque Hempstead, tonight's opponent, I can tell that the team's focus is elsewhere. I thought this might happen, so I had a backup plan to help the girls relax.

"Before we go out on the court tonight, I thought you

could all use a little magic," I say to them. I walk over to the door and stick my head through the opening, "Hey Ernie, we're ready for you."

Earlier this week, I'd asked Ernie if he would come talk to the girls prior to the match. He hesitated a moment before agreeing. I knew this wouldn't be easy for him, but he was willing to put his own emotions aside as a favor to me and more importantly, because of his unwavering commitment to these girls. I barely knew the man prior to this season, and now we have forged an emotional bond that will never be broken. I search for him after every match and we embrace each other without saying a word.

Ernie walks in and the mood in the room immediately shifts from sadness to excitement. The girls gather around as Ernie, an accomplished magician, deftly spreads the cards out on one of the training tables.

"Alright girls," he begins. "Shell, pull out a card, show it to everyone and put it back in the deck. Now shuffle the cards...." He stops midsentence, his voice cracking and his eyes filling with tears.

I grab both his hands. "Ernie, Squeaks always tells me to take a big breath." I look over at her and wink.

Ernie does just that and regains some composure. He pulls off three mind-bending tricks and the girls squeal with delight. When he finishes his final card trick, he tells the girls to have fun and play the way that only West High can. He hugs each senior and then we all go out to the gym.

The volleyball officials meet with the coaches and captains to determine which team will serve first, and the two teams begin warm-ups. Scott places Caroline's shoes under the empty first chair, and I put a Spiderman mask a student has given me above the shoes.

Because this is going to be such an emotional night, I've changed our warm-up music. Instead of our normal medley of current Top 10 hits, I cued "The Macarena,"

"YMCA" and "Tip Toe Through the Tulips," to lighten the mood. Our students seem to enjoy the change and they're dancing away in the bleachers, but my players don't seem to notice. They're lost in their own thoughts.

The seventeen-minute warm-up time passes much too quickly. The time has come to honor our seven seniors: Kelley Fliehler, Olivia Fairfield, Caroline Hartman, Hannah Infelt, Olivia Mekies, Anna Pashkova, Shelly Stumpff, as well as manager Cat Rebelskey. The girls are introduced in alphabetical order and a younger teammate escorts each of them over to Scott and me. We hand them each a yellow rose and a certificate of recognition, and give each of them a heart-felt hug. Then they walk out to the middle of the volleyball court to join their family members.

After the last one, Anna, is introduced, the girls all come back over to Scott and me and I give them a white rose. With tears streaming down their faces, they hold hands and walk out to Ernie, who's standing by himself. They hand him Caroline's rose and encircle him in a group hug and the spectators in the gym rise in unison and give a standing ovation. Almost everyone is crying, including many of the Hempstead players and fans.

Now the match is finally ready to begin. Hempstead, coached by Randy Dolson, is ranked fourth in the state and will be a formidable opponent. It seems odd to have one more regular season conference match after we've already played for the overall conference tournament championship only three days earlier, but that's how the schedule is done each year. We easily beat Hempstead 2 - 0 in the quarterfinals of that tournament, but that match won't have any effect on tonight's outcome. Both of our teams are undefeated in our division of the conference, and tonight's match will determine the regular season champions. I have a feeling we're in for a battle.

We overcame early deficits in the first two sets, and prevail 25-22 and 25-18 in the best-of-five format. I hope we can sweep the match by winning the third set because Senior Night has taken an emotional toll on my players. They're giving me everything they have, but their energy levels are waning. I doubt my girls are physically capable of playing a long match.

My fears are realized: Hempstead roars back behind their all-state hitter, Audrey Reeg, and win the next two sets 25-20 and 25-21 to knot the best of five series at 2-2. My players are exhausted, and this is the worst possible scenario in volleyball: allowing an opponent to come back from a 0-2 deficit. Now Hempstead has all the momentum going into the fifth set.

I turn in the lineup for the final set and go join Scott and the girls in the stairwell. This is where we always go between sets for our home matches as there are fewer distractions here and less noise.

Kelley has been tight the entire night and it's affected her setting. She and Eunice have not been connecting, so Hempstead has only had to worry about slowing down Shelly's hits. Somehow I have to get Kelley and Eunice refocused. Right now I know they're worrying about losing instead of focusing on our execution and running our offense.

"This is not acceptable volleyball," I say with a raised voice. "Squeaks, Anna, and Shelly, you need to give Kelley better passes. No one could possibly run an offense with the balls you're giving her."

Kelley puts her hand on my arm and pulls me back into the gym, away from the rest of the team.

"Brez, I know what you're trying to do, but stop it. Caroline would have gotten to those sets. This is on me. I have to make the plays." She walks back into the stairwell to rejoin her team. Astounded by her declaration, I follow her through the doors and watch her address her friends.

"We're not going to lose this match. Your passes are fine. Hitters, be more vocal and let me know where you want me to put your sets. Tell me if they're too high or too fast. I'll get them to you. Let's go play West volleyball."

With just a moment of hesitation, Shelly yells out "West on nine." And the team runs out to the court as our fans rise to their feet and applaud. Scott and I follow them and I realize this was a breakthrough moment for us: Kelley officially took ownership of the setter's position. The ghost of Line is no longer haunting her.

A Senior Night win and a conference championship will now depend on one fifteen-point game. The two teams battle back and forth with players from both sides making big plays. With the score tied at fifteen, neither team has been able to put the match away with the required two point difference. The teams continue to trade points until we finally take a 19-18 lead. With the West High fans on their feet yelling, Hannah Infelt hits a quick attack from the middle front position and the ball falls on Hempstead's side of the court. Hundreds of spectators rush the floor to celebrate with the team, and "Sweet Caroline" begins to play.

The celebration lasts over thirty minutes. No one seems to want to leave the floor. Finally the spectators begin to leave the gym, and the girls, with their families and friends, make their way to the cafeteria for the Senior Night celebration. A banquet table is filled with sandwiches, chips, and a cake decorated with all their names, including Caroline's.

The mood in the room is subdued despite a tremendous comeback win. I know the girls are teetering on an emotional tightrope. They refuse to enjoy their accomplishments because only one thing matters to them: winning a state championship for Line. I wonder if even that will be enough.

## CHAPTER 31

# IOWA HOMECOMING PARADE

**I**'m riding along on an old hay wagon, throwing bubble gum out to the crowd lining the parade route. It's the University of Iowa Homecoming celebration. Some of my girls sit next to me on prickly straw bales, while others walk beside the wagon. Ernie, pulling our wagon with his 1957 John Deere B tractor, occasionally turns and waves to the cheering throng. Two large green banners decorate the sides of the wagon: one says Iowa City West Volleyball, and the other says 2010 Iowa State Volleyball Champions.

During the past two seasons, Caroline had begged me to let the team participate in the parade on a hay wagon that her dad would pull behind his tractor. I refused. I told her we needed the Friday practice time and besides, we couldn't be on a float unless we had a championship banner to display on the wagon. I then promised her that if we ever won a state championship, we could ride in the parade the following year. Caroline reminded me of that promise last year when we won the state tournament.

As the parade route winds through downtown Iowa City, I know that Line would have been in her glory if she were with us now, dancing around and yelling to the crowd.

The on-lookers are very receptive when we pass by on our float. Their cheers increase noticeably and I see a few people pointing at the banners. Almost everyone in town is familiar with our story. The girls grin and wave at the cheering people.

At the end of the parade, Ernie decides that everyone—the team, their families and friends—should come out to the farm for an impromptu cookout and bonfire. The parents quickly put together a potluck menu.

The nights are becoming brisk now that it's late October. I go home to grab some warmer clothing and pick up Charlie. When I reach the Founds' farm, I'm shocked by the number of people already there. Two men are directing traffic to park in a hay field behind the barn, because there aren't any more spots to park in the driveway. With the help of social media, the word must've spread quickly about a party at the Founds'.

I glance through the open barn doors. A big boom box is playing, and twenty or thirty kids are dancing up in the loft. Unlike at the previous year's celebration, I'm not in the mood to join in the fun. Instead I walk around talking to the players' parents, then go over to the bonfire. Charlie quickly sits down next to me, content to have his ears rubbed.

Mesmerized by the billowing flames, I sit there thinking about the regular season schedule we've just finished. Any other year, a 34-6 record and the top ranking in the state would be cause for celebration. Every single day is hard for my players. In their minds, Line was West High volleyball. Now every time they step on the court, for practice or a match, it's a painful reminder that she's gone. Volleyball isn't fun; it's work. I'm not doing a good enough job of helping them relax and have fun.

I snap out of it when I realize that my players have made their way over to the bonfire. All the girls are sitting in a circle staring quietly into the fire, lost in their own thoughts. Only the players and their families are now still at the farm, everyone else has left.

I look at my girls' solemn faces and I feel sad that

they've lost their youthful innocence, that their joyful expectations for their senior year have been shattered.

"I have an idea," I say. "Let's go into the barn and tell ghost stories."

They groan and make faces like this is the stupidest idea in the history of the world, the way all teenagers do when an adult makes a suggestion. But despite their show of annoyance, they get up off the bales and we walk to the barn. We enter the renovated area, formerly a grain bin, and sit on the floor in a tight circle, Charlie on one side of me and Squeaks on the other. With all the lights off, we can only see each other's silhouettes.

The girls tell several scary stories of their own: psycho-killers who prey on babysitting teenagers or couples making out in cars. Finally it's my turn to scare everyone.

"My story is actually a true one. When I lived in Wisconsin, I had a stalker. I would come home from playing in a softball tournament, only to discover that someone had spent the weekend in my house. One time the Sunday newspaper was strewn all over the living room, another time, all the food in my refrigerator was eaten and the dirty dishes had been left on the counter and stove top. Another time every single light bulb in my house was unscrewed. I lived alone, so you can imagine how frightened I was."

"Well, what happened next?" Squeaks asks. "Did you move away from town?"

"I finally got angry and decided I'd had enough. I was going to protect myself. I bought a Doberman pinscher named Josh and kept my dad's .410 shotgun next to my bed. One night, Josh's low threatening growl woke me up. I peeked through the slats between my bedroom blinds, and saw someone pouring gasoline on the outside wall of my house. I called the police, but then I realized they wouldn't get to my house in time, so I grabbed the shotgun with my right hand and Josh's collar with my left hand. With the loaded gun, I tiptoed to the kitchen door..."

Suddenly there's a noise at the other side of the barn: rusty hinges creaking as a door is slowly pushed open. Whoever's coming through the door switches on a flashlight and the light illuminates the length of a shotgun barrel. Charlie begins to growl. The girls all scream and I almost scream too, but then it occurs to me that it has to be Ernie. I knew he kept a shotgun in the barn to chase out pigeons, and I knew that, as a prankster, nothing would amuse him more than to give the girls a good playful scare. I grab Squeaks and pull her body in front of mine. She struggles to get out of my grip, but I hold her tightly. It's absolute bedlam, the girls screaming and Charlie barking. Then the overhead lights come on and Ernie steps into the room. The look of surprise on the players' faces is absolutely priceless. Their expressions range from relief to disbelief.

I'm laughing so hard I lose my grip on Squeaks. She turns around and punches me in the shoulder. "You used me as a *human shield!*" she yells. "I can't believe you would sacrifice me to *save yourself!*" She and the rest of the players march indignantly out of the barn.

Ernie explains to me that when he came over to the barn to grab some firewood, he overheard my tale. Improvising, he decided to add a little more drama to my story. The three of us laugh so hard we can barely stand up. It's the first time any of us have laughed this hard since August and it feels great.

I never did get to tell the girls the end of the story: that I ran out the door to confront the man beside my house, but he took off and got into a waiting car down the block. After several more frightening incidences, a local police officer said it wasn't safe for me to even go out for a jog alone on the rural roads of Cuba City, WI. I had enough, and not long after that, I made the decision to leave the area and attend graduate school in Iowa City.

## CHAPTER 32

# LIVE LIKE LINE: COMPASSION

I'm sitting in a classroom with my colleagues from the Valley division on Sunday, October 16th. Every year, when the regular season ends, the Mississippi Valley Conference coaches get together at Linn Mar High School in Marion, Iowa, and we vote for all-conference awards and discuss possible changes to our by-laws. Because our conference has too many schools to play each other, the fourteen teams are divided into two divisions: the Valley and the Mississippi.

It's always nice to see everyone, but the atmosphere can get tense as coaches campaign for their athletes. Nine of our fourteen conference teams are currently in the state rankings, so there are many highly skilled athletes to choose from for postseason honors. Ten athletes will receive first-team recognition and ten will make the second-team. Two additional athletes from each school will receive honorable mention all-conference. These awards are very competitive and very political. In 2010 one of our players, Lexi Potter, was actually named the state Player of the Year, but still wasn't voted onto the first team for all-conference.

Each coach nominates one or more of their own athletes for first-team all-conference consideration. When the nomination process is complete, each coach picks ten players and writes their names on a slip of paper. The top ten vote-getters receive first-team honors and the same procedure is repeated for second-team.

We've won the Valley division title as well as our fourteen-team conference tournament, so I know my players will be well represented on the all-conference teams, but I'm troubled. If Caroline had lived she would have been a unanimous first-team selection and a legitimate candidate for Player of the Year.

The votes for first-team are tallied and my throat constricts when I see that Shelly, Olivia Fairfield, and Anna Pashkova make the list. Before nominations begin for the second-team voting, I know there's something I need to do. Turning sideways on my chair, I clear my throat and begin to address the other six coaches in the room: "I have a favor to ask each of you. If Caroline Found was still alive…." I can't go any farther. My eyes fill with tears and I bring my clenched hand up to my mouth. My throat closes. It's impossible to talk. Thankfully I've already told my good friend Barb Sullivan about my plan.

The Xavier coach puts her hand on my arm and says to the group, "What Brez is trying to ask is, would you all be okay with Caroline Found being added as an eleventh player to the first-team all-conference list? Caroline would have been one of the best setters in the state this season and, I believe, she would have been voted Player of the Year in our conference."

I lift my head and see every coach in the room solemnly nod. I quietly tell them thanks. My heart fills with gratitude.

## CHAPTER 33

# LET'S GO TO STATE

We arrive at Jefferson High School for the regional championship game, and Scott and I get off the bus and stand at the bottom of the steps. We high-five each player as she gets off and say, "Don't forget to have fun tonight." Five days earlier, when we beat Des Moines Roosevelt at our last home game at the regionals, the girls were loose and relaxed on the court and, as Scott said, we were "scary good." When I look at their faces tonight, I'm not sure that's the case.

My team and I walk into a quiet Jefferson gym and find our opponent, Cedar Rapids Washington, hasn't arrived yet. We're playing here because the Iowa Girls High School Athletic Association (IGHSAU) schedules regional championship matches at neutral sites in order to be fair to both participating schools. If the games were played in either team's home gym that would give that team an advantage. This way both teams and both teams' fans have to travel, and nobody feels more comfortable than anyone else.

Kelly Phelan, the varsity coach at Jefferson, walks over to me as Scott and I set our briefcases down on the bench. She's been a great friend to me this season, keeping in touch through texts and emails. She gives me a long hug and whispers in my ear, "Best of luck tonight Brez. I know your girls will be awesome." She starts to walk away, then turns back. "Let me know if there's anything I can do for you."

*The only thing I wish anyone could do,* I think, *is*

*impossible. Line is not coming back.*

My girls go into the locker room to change into their uniforms. Fifteen minutes later they return dressed and ready to begin warm-ups. They jog around the court and do their stretches. Normally they would begin to ball-handle now, but the IGHSAU doesn't allow any ball-handling until the game clock shows it's seventeen minutes before the game will start. I check the time, and see we still have thirty minutes before the two game officials call the captains for the coin flip. We've arrived too early and the girls are unsure about what they should do next. Some of them wander over to visit parents and friends, while others talk nervously in small groups.

I hear the Washington team arrive and look over to see their players are laughing and having a good time. This is in stark contrast to my girls, who seem anxious and tense. When I wave a greeting to Washington's head coach, Kari Lombardi, I notice a large floor-waxing machine in the corner and get an idea.

I jump up off the bench. "Seniors, follow me. It's time to ride the Zamboni." As always, my girls look at me like I'm crazy. Finally Olivia Mekies smiles, and I know she's made the connection. A Zamboni is used to resurface the ice in hockey arenas. If we win tonight we'll be playing the state tournament in the Cedar Rapids Ice Arena because of renovations to the US Cellular Center, the normal tournament venue. That has nothing to do with anything in this moment, but I think of it as I run over to the corner of the gym and climb onto the "Zamboni's" driver's seat. The senior girls quickly pile onto the machine's back platform and any other available surfaces. Making tire-screeching noises, I hunch over the steering wheel and pretend we're caroming across the floor. The girls' parents quickly come over to take pictures, and judging by my players' goofy grins and laughter, I know they're much looser now than they were five minutes earlier.

Tonight's match with Washington concerns me. Kari's

a great coach and I know she'll have an effective game plan and her team will be well prepared. The Washington players will be confident because we only barely beat them two weeks ago in the conference tournament.

The officials call both teams' coaches and captains over to the scorer's table for the pre-match rules meeting. We all introduce ourselves and shake hands. I wink at Kari because the two us have gone through this ritual many times. The referee for the match begins to discuss the ground rules for the Jefferson gymnasium and my mind wanders. I look at my captains—Kelley, Shelly, Hannah, Eunice, Anna, and Squeaks—and smile. I can't imagine that any coach has been prouder of his or her players than I am at this moment. Even if we lose the match tonight I'll always admire and love these young women and everyone else on the team.

Washington has the serve to start the match and we quickly get into a rhythm. Squeaks passes Kelley a perfect ball and Hannah hits a quick set from the middle of the net. The ball slams to the floor and my players leap with excitement; Shelly pumps both her fists and Anna gives a yell. I've been very nervous about this match, but my fears are quickly allayed. My players have immediately asserted their dominance on the court and I know that tonight we're going to be unbeatable.

We win the first two sets by the scores of 25 – 12 and 25 – 10.

We get a comfortable lead in the third set and I have no doubts about the outcome of this match. Our post-season is not going to end tonight. I lean back in my seat and enjoy watching my girls on the court. I think about how far they've come in the past ten weeks. Playing with poise and confidence, and they look like a well-oiled machine making precision passes, playing stellar defense, and hitting unpassable shots. In particular, I'm so proud of Kelley and how far she has come. She's absorbed everything I've tried to teach her about setting. Without any previous experience, she's developed into a quality setter. She makes great decisions on the court, sets a perfect ball, and has quietly evolved into a floor leader.

What she's accomplished this season is nothing short of miraculous.

It takes less than an hour for us to sweep Cedar Rapids Washington, and when the final point goes up on the scoreboard, Scott squeezes my hand. I look at him. The tears in his eyes mirror mine, and I shake my head in wonderment. If someone had come up to me on August 12th, when we were sitting with hundreds of devastated kids in West High's darkened gym, and told me that we would be in this position on November 1st, I would have told them they were crazy. The girls soldiered on this season despite their pain. It's every team's dream to qualify for the state tournament. I can hardly believe we've done it.

The Jefferson athletic director presents my girls with a triangular green state tournament banner to hang in our gym and gives medals to each of the players. When I'm walking over to join my team for pictures I overhear Kari, the Washington coach, tell a reporter, "West High is a good team but they had that whole emotion thing going for them." Her comment gives me pause. My girls won in spite of their emotions, not because of them. I like Kari and I know she isn't being disrespectful of my girls, but *no one* will ever know what it was like on our practice court every night this season.

Kelly Phelan comes over and congratulates me. I say, "Kell, I do have a favor to ask of you. Would you mind asking your deejay to play Sweet Caroline for us?"

"I'd be more than happy to," she says.

Kelly walks over to the Jefferson deejay and within seconds our adopted theme song fills the gymnasium. Our smiles shine brightly while the cameras click away, my girls proudly holding up the state tournament banner and Caroline's jersey.

## CHAPTER 34

# LIVE LIKE LINE: OUTRAGEOUS HUMOR

It's 2:45 on Thursday, November 3rd, and I'm frantically searching for a cowboy outfit at Goodwill. One day last year, Caroline announced that Thursday was going to be Theme Day for practices. On Wednesdays she would tell everyone what to wear to practice the next day. It could be anything from crazy socks to all black or all white clothing. Thursday August 10th, the day before she died, was neon day. Line wore bright yellow socks, a neon pink shirt and a green headband. I awarded her with a $10 gift certificate to Panchero's for the best outfit.

But Theme Day, like our warm-up music, was abandoned when we lost her. In mid-September, Scott reinstituted it. After that, he texted everyone every Wednesday about what to wear to practice the following day. Yesterday I received a text from Shelly telling me that tomorrow's practice was Western Day. I don't know why it's coming from Shelly instead of Scott, but it doesn't matter. I'm still running up and down the aisles of Goodwill thirty minutes before practice.

I seldom participate in Theme Day, because either I don't have the right clothes, or I don't bother taking the time to put an outfit together. But if we lose in the first round of the state tournament, this will be the last Thursday practice of the season, so I've decided to surprise the team and dress the part.

I find a cowboy hat in one aisle, a western-style plaid shirt, complete with fake pearl snaps in another aisle, and a pair of worn cowboy boots that don't fit me. I barely get to school before the start of practice. I feel resplendent as I tuck my new cowboy shirt into the waistband of my Levis. I pull the cowboy hat low over my brow and saunter into the gym in my two-sizes-too-big cowboy boots.

The players are already jogging for warm-ups, and as soon as they see my attire they begin to laugh. They laugh so hard that some of them drop to the floor, clutching their sides. I can't figure out what they think is so funny and then I take a closer look at them: not one of them is wearing any western clothing. *What the heck?* I think.

When the girls finally regain their composure, Shelly jogs past me and says, "Welcome to Dress-Like-Brez Day."

Scott is bent over laughing and doesn't notice me coming toward him until I'm by his side. I push him as hard as I can with both of my hands. "Thanks a lot, buddy. I'm sure glad to know you have my back." He continues to laugh as I turn away.

I try to ignore the girls but my curiosity gets the best of me. What does dressing like Brez look like? I look around and see that all the girls have their t-shirts tucked into baggy shorts that drape down to their knees. Several have whistles around their necks and Shelly is sporting two huge pillows stuffed into the upper part of her shirt. I'm speechless. It's acutely humbling to see yourself through the eyes of a bunch of seventeen-year-olds.

Just when I think things can't get any worse, I hear, "Coach, can we go ahead and get that interview now?" I slowly turn around to see a reporter and camera crew standing by the entrance to the gym. I completely forgot that one of the local television stations was coming in to shoot some footage for tonight's broadcast. I sheepishly remove my cowboy hat and feebly run my hand through the sweat-soaked hair that's plastered to my head. Great, I think. Not only have I lost complete credibility with my team, but now it's going to be recorded for the rest of eastern Iowa to see as well.

I gamely try to get through the interview while ignoring my players making faces at me from behind the cameraman. When the reporter leaves, I bark at the girls to get started with practice.

Shelly takes the pillows out of her shirt and the girls start ball-handling, still snickering and looking proud of themselves. I watch them, still feeling embarrassed and a little irritated at myself that I let them one-up me. Then something occurs to me that makes me smile. This is a stunt Line would have pulled off.

Live like Line.

## CHAPTER 35
# BUTTERFLIES

There's an entire week between the regional championship and the quarterfinals of the state tournament. It's a difficult time to plan practices. You don't want your players to get rusty during the break, but high intensity practice drills increase the risk of injury. It's important to keep a healthy balance between working on individual skills and doing competitive drills.

This is our fifth consecutive year to qualify for the state tournament, and through trial and error I've found what works best for us. We never have practice the day after we win the regional finals. This gives my players time to reenergize. Wednesday and Thursday we have regular practices and today, Friday, Tom Keating comes down to talk to the team.

Tom is the Cedar Rapids principal and former Wahlert coach who told me, the day after Caroline died, that volleyball was going to help the girls and me get through this, and that I shouldn't give up on the season. There are some coaches that would be uncomfortable asking another coach to motivate his or her players, but I don't feel that way. Tom has a great volleyball mind and with his degree in psychology, he's an incredible motivator. I like having him talk to my teams in the post-season and he's always willing to help us out. Sometimes I think that after listening to Tom talk for thirty minutes, I'd be pumped-up enough to run through a brick wall for him. I know he has the same effect on my girls.

First the team and I go to my Health Education classroom and watch game film of our first-round opponent, Council Bluffs Abraham Lincoln High School, as we wait for Tom's arrival. When scouting a volleyball opponent, you analyze their tendencies in game situations: which player is most likely to get set in each rotation, the team's defensive patterns and weaknesses in serve reception. Scouting an unknown opponent is as important as practicing on the court.

When we're almost done watching film, I see Tom standing in the hall outside my classroom. I go out and greet him. I thank him for coming and we joke around for a couple minutes. Then Tom's expression turns serious. "I need to know if it's okay to talk about Caroline. Are your girls going to be all right if I mention her?"

I assure him that the players will be open to anything he has to say.

We walk in the room and I introduce him to the girls. The returning players know Tom because he spoke to the team last season, but I go through his credentials for the new players: eleven state championships as the coach at Dubuque Wahlert High School, eleven-time state volleyball coach of the year, and one-time national coach of the year. The girls lean forward in their seats, full of anticipation.

Tom congratulates them on a great season and on overcoming so many hardships together. "And don't let anyone tell you that you've had this success because you have an emotional edge. That's crap," he says. "You're in this position because you've worked your butts off every day in practice and you've earned your spot in the state tournament. You're in this position because you've worked harder than every single other team in the state."

It takes everything I have to not laugh out loud when Tom says that, because of how little we've practiced this season.

He talks about motivation, preparation, and the pressure that comes with being one of the teams favored to win the state championship. Then he begins to talk about nerves. "It would be crazy to think you're not going to be nervous, especially this season. I know how much pressure you've put on yourselves. You've dealt with unbelievable expectations all season. You will get butterflies in your stomach before you step on the court. Well, here's what you need to do. Take those butterflies and make them work for you. Put them in formation and make them fly away. All you have to remember is that if *you* have butterflies, think how those girls in the other locker room must feel. They have to play Iowa City West!"

Tom talks for a little while longer, but my mind is elsewhere. I'm getting an idea about how to make sure those dang butterflies work in our favor.

## CHAPTER 36

# STATE TOURNAMENT QUARTERFINALS

I'm having breakfast with my team at the Coralville HyVee grocery store. We're eating together before leaving for Cedar Rapids and our state tournament quarterfinals match. Eadie Fawcett from the University of Iowa Community Credit Union has joined us. Our local banks do a tremendous job recognizing student and athletic achievement. Hills Bank always has a reception for the players and families of state qualifying teams, and the Credit Union provides breakfast on the day of the state tournament. Before we arrived, she decorated our seating area with banners, flowers, and goody bags for the kids. She congratulates the girls and tells them how proud the entire community is of the season they've had.

My players are a little goofy. I watch them hit balloons at each other and talk too loud, and know this is their way of coping with stress. I'm nervous as well. Our first round opponent, Council Bluffs Abraham Lincoln, only has a 26-21 record, but what if this might be the match when my girls finally collapse? I'm not concerned that Abe Lincoln can beat us, but I am concerned that we might beat ourselves with unforced errors.

When I stop at the register, Eadie reminds me that the Credit Union is picking up the tab. I thank her and go outside with the rest of the team. It's beginning to rain and the bus is on the other side of the parking lot.

I'm able to get the bus driver's attention and wave him over to where we're standing.

The girls file up the steps and I note nervously that their behavior has changed from jocular to solemn. I start to follow them up the steps and happen to glance down. There on the wet pavement are three pennies, glistening in the rain. I'm astonished. I think of the pennies showing up in the locker room in September, and felt like somehow Caroline had something to do with those pennies showing up as a sign when I needed one the most. Now here they are again. What are the odds that the bus would have pulled up right in the spot where there were three pennies on the ground? I've watched every person on my team get on the bus and none of them could have put those pennies on the ground for me to find. Besides, I haven't told anyone about the penny incident in the locker room last month.

I feel a calmness settle over me as I pick up the pennies. I'll make sure I tape them inside the Spiderman mask we always keep on the empty first chair, before we play today. I shut my eyes for a moment and silently thank Line for letting me know that things are going to be okay.

It's only a short twenty-five minute ride to the Cedar Rapids Ice Arena and one of the state officials greets us as soon as we walk in the door. He escorts the girls to our locker room and I turn to Scott and Ashten and say, "Hey, let's go check out the arena while the girls are changing." We've never been in this venue before, and I'm curious about the layout of the playing court and spectator seating.

There's a large practice ice rink to the left of the main foyer. I can see the girls walking down a hallway that runs parallel to it. Scott, Ashten, and I cross the atrium and step into the main ice arena. We stop and stare. It's a beautiful setting for volleyball. Unlike in the US Cellular Center, where the championships are normally played, the bleachers in this arena extend all the way to the playing floor. Only a four-foot wall separates the fans from the bench area, just like with ice hockey games. The arena, with a maximum capacity of only 3,800, is a much more intimate environment than the US Cellular venue.

The two playing courts are set up so that their endlines are only thirty feet apart. A large net is suspended from the ceiling and divides the playing areas so the players on the two courts can't interfere with each other. It'll be easy for spectators to watch both courts play simultaneously.

The three of us step out onto the court to check out the playing surface. Other than the temperature being a little cooler than normal, you'd never know that inches below the portable rubberized-finish court is a semi-professional ice hockey rink.

We put our jackets on the backs of our chairs and Scott puts Caroline's shoes under the first chair. When he begins to set the Spiderman mask on the seat I say, "Hey, do you mind taping these on the back of that mask with the others?" I hand him the pennies and he looks at me quizzically. "Don't ask. They're from Caroline. I think she wanted to wish us good luck," I tell him with a smile.

The three of us start walking down the hallway to join our team in the locker room. Then it occurs to me that we don't have any idea what locker room we've been assigned to. I look at Ashten and Scott. "We've lost the team," I say. "Do either of you know which one of these four locker rooms was assigned to us?"

They both shake their heads. They have no idea.

We walk into the first locker room and interrupt our opponents' preparing for the match. Embarrassed, I apologize, and we step back into the hallway. I turn to my coaches. "Well, that was a little awkward. Any suggestions on how we should find our team?"

Scott looks at me and says, "We yell!"

He and Ashten start yelling "West" as loud as they

can, and the sound of their voices echoes off the walls of the rink. The few skaters on the ice in the practice area stare at us. We begin to laugh because the fact that we can't find our players is ridiculous. For some reason Scott and Ashten yelling *"West, West"* reminds me of Marlon Brando yelling up to the window of the room where his wife is hiding in the movie "Streetcar Named Desire." and I cup my hands around my mouth and start yelling, *"Stella! Stella!"*

The three of us walk past two more locker room entrances and Scott and Ashten continue to yell for West while I continue to yell for Stella. We're having such a good time we've almost forgotten about the circumstances and the time constraints.

Then Squeaks sticks her head out the last door along the hall. "What is *wrong* with you guys?"

Sheepishly, I look at Scott and Ashten and then I look back at Squeaks. "You don't even want to know."

The three of us join the girls in the cramped locker room. Perspiration's dripping down their faces, so we can tell they've already done their ritual dance. They jump up and down in nervous excitement. I motion them over and they crowd around me. I don't have any super motivational speech prepared; they know what's at stake. Instead, I talk about controlling the tempo of the match and staying focused in the moment. I remind them that being nervous now is natural.

Each year before our first match of the state tournament I try to come up with an idea to help relieve their nerves. Last year, I gave each girl an identical piece of yellow paper and asked them to write down their biggest fear about playing in the state tournament. When they were finished writing, I told them ,"We're going to completely get rid of those fears. Tear your papers into as many pieces as possible and throw them away." The girls began to laugh and enthusiastically tore their individual papers into shreds. With a yell, they all ran out of the locker room, following Caroline as she searched for a garbage can. Later on that day, when our first match was over, I asked Line what she wrote down as her biggest fear. She scrunched up her forehead and answered earnestly, "My biggest fear was that I was going to be afraid during the match and do a terrible job of setting. Once I tore up that paper I wasn't afraid anymore." That memory gives me momentary pause now before I continue talking to my girls.

"I have something for each of you," I say. Earlier in the week I decided to use Tom's nerves and butterflies metaphor to help the girls deal with their fears this time around at State. I made fifteen fist-sized butterflies out of brightly colored construction paper, each one with a different color and style. Now I hand each player a butterfly. Then I place a blank white, two-by-three-foot poster board on the locker room bench.

"We're going to get rid of our butterflies before we step on the court. I want each of you to write down your greatest fear on the wings of your butterflies. What are you most nervous about before this match?"

Scott hands out pens and the girls quickly write their fears on the bottom side of their butterflies' wings.

When the last girl finishes, I say, "Now we're going to put the butterflies on this board in some kind of formation." I watch the girls tape the first six butterflies in a straight line at the bottom of the board. Then, without anyone saying a word, they put the next nine butterflies in a straight line perpendicular to the first line. I choke back my tears when I see what they've done: the butterflies are in the shape of the letter L. I pull a metal butterfly from my pocket and hand it to Kelley. I bought this butterfly at a craft fair last week, for this purpose. It's much larger than the others and is decorated with colorful stones. "This is the butterfly that will always be there when you start to get nervous," I tell the girls. "Kell, put it on the board in whatever you think is the best spot."

Kelley carefully tapes the butterfly to the poster board

at the top of the L. Every player on the team nods her agreement with Kelley's decision. The decorated butterfly is leading all the rest of the butterflies that hold their fears. The girls huddle up and count to nine. As they leave the locker room, each player reaches out and touches the burnished-brown butterfly.

My girls don't look particularly sharp during the game, but I'm not too concerned, because we're playing the way we've played all season: just well enough to get by. I'm confident that we'll do better as the tournament progresses. I can't help but notice how impressive Iowa City High looks on the adjacent court, easily dominating a strong Cedar Falls team. If both City and West win the next match, we'll be on a collision course for the championship.

In the end, we play well enough to beat Abe-Lincoln, 25 – 20, 25 – 15 and 25 - 20. Shelly played particularly well, recording nine kills, three ace serves, and two blocks. She has evolved so much psychologically this season. Last year in the championship match against Ankeny, she made a couple of hitting errors and when she was subbed out for a defensive player she had tears in her eyes. This year I'm not worried about her abilities to take the tension. Without Line, Shelly has emerged as a leader and refuses to let errors affect her game. She's the person that the rest of the girls look to when the pressure is high. She encourages her teammates with pats on the back and cracks jokes to keep everyone – the girls as well as me and Scott – loose during practices and games.

The girls collect the things they'd left on the bench, looking more relieved than excited that they beat Abe-Lincoln and are one more step closer to the state championship. Hundreds of West High students, wearing their bright blue Live Like Line t-shirts, continue standing next to their seats, some of them dancing in the bleachers and cheering the girls on. The song "YMCA" begins to play over the speakers and they enthusiastically contort their bodies into the letters. It's as if our fans don't want to leave the arena.

My girls wave toward the student section and continue vacating the area around the bench to make room for the next team that's coming. The song "YMCA" ends and "Sweet Caroline" begins to play. I don't know if the state volleyball officials intentionally played this song for us, or if it came up randomly in the queue. It doesn't matter; the reaction is electric. My athletes scream, run over to the student section, and all of those kids, the team and the fans begin to sing the song together, tears streaming down their faces.

## CHAPTER 37
# THE LAST PRACTICE

It's Thursday and Scott and I are in my office finishing our game plan for our next match. We'll be playing Cedar Rapids Kennedy tomorrow, and if we win the match we'll be going up against the other state semifinal winner, either Ankeny or City High, for the championship on Saturday.

It seems impossible that this will be our last practice of the year—time has passed so quickly. My team is one of four 5A schools still playing in the state of Iowa. I'm so happy for my girls, but I can't help feeling sad and nostalgic too. This is the last time we'll be together in this gymnasium. We've shared so much. What's it going to be like when we don't have volleyball to hold us together? Even though every practice has been a struggle emotionally, at least we had each other. After this weekend, we'll go our separate ways and things won't ever be the same. I know there's going to be a huge void in my life without these girls. I'm sure the girls feel the same way.

Scott and I enter the gym. My players are on the other side of the court. They're sitting in a circle doing their stretching exercises. They begin to laugh when they see us. Every one of them is wearing an insulated snowmobile suit or ski pants. They tell us that they decided today should be Snow Day. Caroline, for some inexplicable reason, called Scott Snowpants – Snowy for short – and the girls took it upon themselves to recognize Scott for their last Theme Day.

Scott's blushing, but I know he's pleased. The players love him and this is their way of showing their appreciation. I can't help but smile along with them because they look ridiculous. It's an exceptionally warm November day and the girls quickly begin to unzip their outfits, anxious to get out of them.

"Oh wait," I say. "I think it's time to jog. We can't waste any more practice time than we already have."

"What?" Shelly screams. "We can't wear these for practice!"

I try to maintain a serious demeanor as I say sternly, "I'm sure that at this very moment, Kennedy is practicing hard and preparing to beat us. We need to do the same. *Start jogging.*"

The girls moan and begin to lumber around the gym, their arms stiffly held out away from their bodies because of their bulky clothing. I turn to Scott. "They look like Ralphie in the movie "The Christmas Story," the scene when he falls down in the snow and can't get back up because he has so many clothes on." The two of us begin to laugh.

After one lap, I tell the girls they can take their suits off. They're giggly and playful for the remainder of the practice. We really don't get too much accomplished as far as preparing for Kennedy, but I don't care. It's more important to me that they enjoy this practice, the last one for the seniors as members of the West High volleyball team.

## CHAPTER 38

# THE STATE CHAMPIONSHIP SEMI-FINALS

We're standing in the locker room before our match against Cedar Rapids Kennedy. The Cougars will be a formidable opponent—we had a difficult time when we played them in the conference tournament—and they've been ranked in the top five all season. Kennedy is a senior-dominated squad. This will be the third year in a row that we've played them in the state semi-finals, and I know they'll be pumped up to get a win against us this time. Their coach, Michelle Goodall, won't need to remind them that we've eked out wins against them in the state semi-finals during the past two seasons.

There's something I don't need to remind my players of either. Today is November 11th, the three-month anniversary of Caroline's accident. Our locker room is quiet. The girls are lost in their own thoughts. I pull out the poster board and the girls reach for their butterflies. They write down their fears, just like they did before Wednesday's match. When they finish they once again tape their butterflies to the poster board in the shape of a large letter L and Kelley attaches the metal butterfly at the top.

"Okay, listen up," I say. "We know this isn't going to be an easy match. Don't let Kennedy go on long point-scoring runs, remember 'next ball,' and more than anything else, have fun out there. When things get tough, all you have to do is look at the teammate beside you. She has your back."

The girls huddle up, count to nine, and jog out the door to the court. I look at Scott. "Well, what are you thinking?"

"If we control Hutch, we win the match," he says.

Allie Hutcheson is a three-year starter for Kennedy. I've known her mom, Cindy, for years, and whenever I see Allie, I joke with her that she should be playing on my team. I always enjoy watching Allie play. A six-foot-tall, left-handed hitter/setter, she is one of the top players in the state. She poses a particularly difficult match-up, because when she's in the front court, you never know if she's going to set the ball or attack on the second contact. I respect her as a player—she is fiercely competitive and an incredible athlete—but I love her as a person. She has a personality similar to Line's, and people gravitate to her. She's always smiling, always outgoing and positive. She and Line became good friends during the club season. She was the first person to call me on the night of the accident, after I heard the news from Kelley and Shelly, and I know how much she grieved the loss of her friend. But today, none of that will matter. Her sole focus will be on beating us.

The teams begin their thirteen-minute warm-ups and our manager, Cat Rebelskey, comes to me with an unexpected request. "The Kennedy students want to do a 'Live Like Line' chant with our students," she says. "Should they do it before or after the match?"

I turn and look at the Kennedy crowd standing and cheering eight feet behind our bench. Many of their faces are painted green and gold, and several young men are standing together with letters on their bare chests spelling out "Kennedy." Then I see it: One of the Kennedy fans has draped a "Live Like Line" t-shirt over the railing in front of their student section.

I'm taken aback by this simple act of sportsmanship. No matter how bad both teams want to win today, it's still just a game. I turn to Cat, "It would probably be better to do it before the match," I say. "If we wait until after the match, one of our teams is going to be crying and broken-hearted. And Cat, please tell them thanks from us."

My girls step on the court for the five-minute warm-up at the net. "Live Like Line," some Kennedy students yell, and from the other side of the arena, our students repeat the phrase. The cheer builds momentum and people from other schools join in until the chant reaches a deafening crescendo. My girls look at each other with small, tight smiles. I can tell they're overwhelmed with emotion.

The match begins and my girls play with passion and confidence. We dominate the first two sets, winning 25-18 in both games. Kennedy looks rattled. We lead 23 to 21 in the third set. We're only two points away from sweeping the match, but then the wheels come off. Allie Hutcheson rotates to the front court and gets four consecutive kills. Kennedy wins the third set, 25-23.

I feel good going into the fourth set. Except for our small meltdown at the end of the third game, we've looked good. The teams take the court and the Kennedy girls, particularly Hutcheson, pick up right where they left off at the end of the previous set. They play with confidence and poise, whereas my girls are tentative and demoralized. I use my two timeouts to try to settle them down, but to no avail. We get beat, 15-25.

In the sport of volleyball, giving up a two-set lead is the worst possible scenario. We've given Kennedy all the momentum. My girls are looking at each other accusingly when the ball hits the floor. They need to work together and recover their swagger. I pull them off the court to an area under the bleachers, and they stand close to me so they can hear above the noise of the Kennedy crowd. For the first time all season during a match, I raise my voice at them.

"Listen. We might get beat, but we're not quitting! Not

now, not today. Don't do this to yourselves," I yell. "Stop complaining on the court! Quit blaming each other for mistakes! For God's sake, if we don't have each other's backs, then we don't have a chance." I'm angry and they know it. They quickly huddle and jog back onto the court with looks of determination on their faces.

The deciding set is only a fifteen-point game, so it's imperative to establish an early lead. My girls now look like a completely different team than they did during the last two sets. Shelly controls Hutch at the net and Eunice and Hannah dominate from the middle front position. We quickly grab a 9-4 lead and Kennedy can't answer. We finish the match with a decisive 15-7 victory. We'll be playing City High tomorrow in the state championship match.

The two teams come together at the net and shake hands. Then the celebrating begins. The Russian is at the front of the line, and when she finishes hand-shaking, she throws her arms up, leaps into the air, and screams with joy. The girls throw themselves on each other. All the seniors are crying with happiness and relief—mostly relief, I think. What got them through the season was the thought of succeeding for Caroline. From day one, their goal was to win the state championship, as improbable and unrealistic as that seemed to me. They almost lost to Kennedy tonight, but they didn't. And now they're one game away from winning state. But they'll have to beat our archrival, Iowa City High, to do it.

In the stands the West High students, wearing purple Team Ellyn shirts, are dancing and screaming. I look over at Ernie, standing in the bleachers in the middle of the parents' section. Everyone around him is hugging him and clapping him on the back. Our eyes meet, I give him a thumbs up, and he smiles. I know he feels the same way I do: satisfied that we've won, relieved on the girls' behalf, and sad that Caroline, who would have basked in this limelight as much as anyone, isn't here today.

## CHAPTER 39

# LIVE LIKE LINE:
# RISE TO THE OCCASION

I'm standing on the sidelines of the Cedar Rapids Ice Arena watching my players warm up for the championship match. In the bleachers West High students, wearing their Live Like Line shirts, outnumber City High students by two-to-one. The atmosphere is electric. The two student sections are taunting each other with good-natured cheers and everyone is on their feet. Today is Shelly's eighteenth birthday, and her friends in the stands start singing "Happy Birthday" to her, and all the other West students join in.

Volleyball reigns supreme in eastern Iowa; six of the eight 5A schools that qualified for the state tournament are from eastern Iowa, the Mississippi Valley conference. Playing against ranked schools every week helped us get to the place we are now. What's even more amazing to me is that today two teams from the same town are playing for a state title. This is the first time in the history of Iowa high school volleyball that this has ever happened. What a tribute to the Iowa City school system, to its athletes, administrators, and club volleyball programs. I'm bursting with pride as I look at the thousands of Iowa Citians sitting in the stands.

The double court that's been used this week for the preliminary matches has been changed to a single court in the center of the arena. The front court area on both sides of the net is red and the back court area on both sides is blue. The out-of-bounds areas are in contrasting colors to the panels next to them. The whole court is colorful, and it should be easy for players and officials to determine whether a ball is landing in-or out-of-bounds.

The horn sounds to end warm-ups and the two teams line up on opposite end lines, facing each other. City High's reserve players and then their starters are introduced, and each girl is greeted with a roar from the Little Hawk contingent. I watch the Little Hawk players, hoping to see signs of nervousness, but their body language and facial expressions exude nothing but confidence.

I beam as my players are introduced. This is what they've waited for all season and I'm so proud of them. The starters are introduced in numerical order. When the announcer says "#11 Shelly Stumpff," Shelly steps forward and pretends she's shooting guns with both hands. I shake my head and smile because that's exactly the kind of showboating Caroline would have done.

I know what this match means to my players, to our students, and our community. Winning this match today would be a way to honor Line, but it would be more than that too. Everyone has used this volleyball team as a means of keeping part of Caroline alive. Our success has enabled people to relive the joy, passion, and spontaneity that Line embodied every day of her life. I can't imagine the pressure my players must be feeling at this moment. I can only hope that, regardless of whether we win or lose, my girls will walk away from this match knowing they played as well as they could.

My heart is pounding as the official extends his arm and signals the serve. I blow out a long breath to calm myself. Here we go—West High versus City High for the state championship. City sends the ball over, and Anna Pashkova passes the ball five feet off the court. Kelley is able to run it down but after a couple rallies, City scores on a huge hit from Michaela Nelson. This is not how I hoped we'd begin the match. We settle down enough to take an early 11-5 lead, but I don't like what I'm seeing on the court. Anna continues to struggle in serve receive and that limits Kelley's setting options. Hannah, Laynie, and Eunice aren't closing their blocks, and the City High's hitters begin to score points by hitting off my blockers' hands. Our early lead quickly fades away and the City High fans erupt when the Little Hawks take their first lead of the set at 23-22. Two big kills by Michaela Nelson seal the win for City High. We're down one set to nothing.

My girls gather around Scott and me. We talk to them about closing the block and settling down on serve receive. I want them to focus on volleyball fundamentals, and not worry about what's at stake. I have no idea how my players will respond to being down. This is the first time all season we've lost the first set of a match against City High. My girls certainly aren't as loose and goofy as they were before the match started.

Both teams begin to play much better volleyball in the second set. Pashkova ignites our team with some huge defensive digs on hits that should've hit the floor. Whitehead and Infelt are getting solid touches on almost every City spike attempt, and Fairfield and Stumpff hit some impressive kills. But we can't pull away; City answers every challenge. Eight times the teams exchange leads and now, close to the end of the set, the score is tied for the sixth time at 23 all. City pulls ahead, 24 to 23, but they miss the serve. We finally get the chance to win at 25-24, but we miss the serve as well. I feel helpless. I don't have any time-outs remaining to calm my players down. *We need to win this set.* Two more times we have set point but we can't finish. Finally, City takes a one-point lead and I watch in disbelief when they ace serve us for a 29-27 victory.

I can't believe that we're down two sets to none.

My players walk off the court in a stupor. It's like they've just witnessed a puppy being run over. The City High players are screaming with excitement. The City High fans are jumping with jubilation. Our fans sit quietly in their seats.

*This can't possibly be happening,* I think. We needed to win one of those first two sets. I know our chances of winning the championship now are slim. City is playing too well and a 0-2 deficit is going to be too hard to overcome. "Please God," I silently pray. "Don't let these girls get swept 0–3. Please just let us win this next set or they'll never forgive themselves." We go off to the side of the bleachers. I have to do something to instill some confidence in my team, even if I don't have any myself.

To my surprise, the girls look more resolute and determined than I've seen them all season—they don't seem defeated at all. I gather them in closer. "Okay, not a big deal. We need to start communicating better on the floor and get more touches at the net. The other times we beat them it was because we controlled the net. Let's start this match over. Pretend we're playing a best-of-three match and the losing team has to put the equipment away." They smile as most of our practices involve the losing team putting the volleyball equipment away at the end. "We need to get some stops on their hitters and win the long rallies. Let's go West, this is our match!"

When we put our hands together to end the huddle, Hannah says matter-of-factly, "There is no way in hell we are losing this match." The players all look at her and nod. I hope they feel more confident than I do.

The City High players are already on the court. They're jumping up and down with excitement and anticipation. They know they'll win this match. On the City High bench, Craig Pitcher and his staff are trying to suppress their smiles. I don't blame them, I'd be feeling the same way if I was in their position.

The set begins much the way the third one finished,

with City taking control. I can only sit on the bench and watch as we fall behind 3 to 6. Shelly makes a couple of hitting errors, and City High's Nelson, only a sophomore, records five kills in City's first ten points. We need a spark, and we get it from the most unlikely duo: Hannah and Laynie. Shelly and Eunice have been our superstars all season and Hannah and Laynie have been role-players, but not today. They block City's hitters three consecutive times, and all of a sudden my players seem to come alive. Eunice rotates up to the net and keeps the momentum going. She gets a solo block and follows with a monster kill on the next play.

My girls begin to get excited and I can tell they're regaining their court swagger. The two teams are tied at 15. Then Pashkova digs a huge swing by Nelson and the rout is on. Four kills from Shelly and a solo block from Laynie propel us to a 25-16 win. My players are smiling as they jog off the court. They have the momentum now.

The fourth set begins, and once again City jumps out to an early lead. We are down 6 to 9, but Pashkova comes through for us. City High's Abby Saehler hits the ball so hard the smack of her hand on the leather resonates throughout arena. The ball heads straight for the floor. Neither of our blockers gets a hand on it and it seems destined to make the point, but somehow the Russian gets her forearms under it, inches before it lands. We win the point with a kill from Shelly, and the players on the court all run over and pat Anna on the back. I don't know it at the time, but her effort on that hit by Saehler is about to change the entire momentum of that game. Laynie, Eunice, and Hannah begin to stop every Little Hawk attack and the City hitters become frustrated. They can't get any hits across the net. I've never seen our front court dominate this way. Their nine blocks push us out front, 21-15. Three kills from Shelly and one more solo block from Laynie give us a 25-17 win.

Scott and I high-five. The officials call both teams'

captains over to the score bench for the coin flip. We win the toss for the fifth and deciding set, and elect to receive serve. Scott stands next to me as I write out our lineup, turn it in, and we walk over to join the girls on one side of the bleachers. City had us on the ropes, but somehow we've fought back. We're all feeling confident.

We huddle up, but there's not much I can say to the girls that they haven't heard before. "This is what we've trained for all year—to be in this position. You know what you have to do to be successful." I watch the girls run back to our bench. It's in their hands now.

"West on nine," Shelly yells, and for the final time of the season—for the final time, period—the team answers with, "One, two, three, four, five, six, seven, eight, nine WEST!" My players jog onto the court and do their superstitious handshakes and body slams. As I watch them, I remember Caroline's pregame ritual: After the official checked the lineup, she would run over to our bench, Scott would stretch his arm up, and she would jump and hit her forehead against his palm.

Both teams play well at the start of the set. Every time Fairfield or Stumpff get a nice kill, Abby Saehler or Nelson do the same for City. Slowly, we start to gather some momentum. Mekies and Pashkova pass every ball perfectly, and Kelley is running a faster offense than we have all season. We're ahead 9 to 6 and then City hits a ball out-of-bounds, and my players scream and jump around, celebrating their 10-6 lead. Then Jay Grassley, the head official, blows his whistle and signals touch. The point goes to City High—the line judge has ruled that our blockers touched the ball before it went out of bounds. Instead of us having a 10-6 lead, the score is now 9 to 7.

On the next play, Hannah hits a ball that ricochets off a City High block before landing off the court, but the signal from the official is "no touch/point City." My players are frustrated and I can see them questioning the official. "Hey," I yell over the crowd noise. "Forget about it. *Next ball!*" This is the exact scenario we've talked about all season. When the point is over, good or bad, move on. We need to focus on the next ball, not on the play that is already over.

Now, as we cling to a 9-8 lead, Shelly rises up in the air to hit. Instead of swinging hard, she drops her elbow and the ball gently rolls over the net and falls toward the floor behind the City High blockers. Erin Muir dives toward the ball that's only inches off the floor and slides her hand across the court surface in an attempt to pancake the ball back up into the air. The ball bounces up in the air and City sends it to the back of our court where it falls untouched. Point City.

I jump off the bench and approach the official on the court. "Didn't you see the ball touch the floor before the City player got her hand under it?"

She tells me she didn't see the play. I look over at Jay, standing on the officials' stand. It's too loud for him to hear me, so I put my hands up over my eyes. This is a universal sign in volleyball that means an official can't make a call because his or her vision has been blocked from the action. Jay shakes his head; he's positive he made the correct call. I'm livid. Three consecutive calls have gone against us. Instead of having a commanding 12-6 lead, we're now tied with City, 9-9. Jay's a decent official and I can see that he's adamant that he's made the correct calls. I'm equally certain that he didn't. There's absolutely nothing that can be done to change the calls now. I need to get both myself and my players refocused. "Forget about it. Next ball," I yell, more for myself than my girls.

Shelly Stumpff hits several nice kills, but each time Michaela Nelson answers for City High and the match is tied at 10. Even though neither of our teams can score two consecutive points and gather enough momentum to seal the victory, it feels to me like City is on the verge of taking control of the match. But what happens next is unfathomable. The Little Hawk players have a complete mental breakdown.

Michaela Nelson goes back to serve and the ball goes long. We're tied 11-11. Shelly sends a tough jump serve over to City, but Rachel Rinehart hits the ball off our block for the point, and she calmly walks back behind the City High endline to put the ball in play. Her serve is so wide it almost hits me as I stand in front of our bench. The two teams are tied for the sixth time in this set, at 12 points each.

Kelley Fliehler serves and City wins the point when the officials call Eunice for a net foul. City has taken a 13-12 lead and are two points away from securing the championship.

I call timeout. I want to calm down my team and hopefully give the next City High server, Abby Saehler, more time to worry about the importance of her serve.

"We need to give Kelley a good pass. Mollie, come in for the quick attack to draw their block and Kelley, I want you to set Eunice a 31." The girls nod in agreement and jog out to the court.

The official signals for serve, but once again City can't perform the most basic of volleyball skills: making a serve. Abby's served ball drops only a few inches behind our endline and we're tied for the seventh time at 13 - 13. If City High could make their serves, the match would be over. I pace on the sideline—I can't believe what I'm seeing. I hear Scott, sitting behind me on the bench, say, "Caroline, do you have to make it so obvious?"

I grin at him.

City can't make a serve, but we can't capitalize on their ineptness. They side out every time we serve to them. Liz Huebring gets a kill for City and they take a 14 to 13 lead. They're only one point away from the state championship. The City High fans are all standing in anticipation of their victory. I can barely watch as Erin Muir tosses the ball up in the air to serve. This could be the end of our season. My girls are going to be heartbroken. Erin mis-hits the ball and her serve hits the bottom of the net. The match is tied at 14-14. I feel terrible for Erin, but I'm ecstatic for my team. We still have a chance.

Twice we take the lead and serve for the championship, but both times Nelson gets a kill to tie the match. Caitlyn Ward misses the fifth City High serve in six attempts and we try for the championship point for the third time. The Russian calmly steps behind the serving line and sends a bullet over the net. City handles the serve and Erin Muir sends a great set out to Abby Saehler on the far side of the court. Saehler nails a big hit down the line that Mollie Mason barely digs up in the air. Kelley runs fifteen feet off the net and simply throws the set all the way across the court to Shelly on the outside. I crouch down on one knee near our endline. The ball will be coming over Shelly's hitting shoulder, and she's going to have an impossible angle. She adjusts her approach to the net and contacts the ball on its right side to make it spin toward the sideline. This is very similar to a billiards player putting "English" on a pool ball. "Oh Shelly, what a terrible decision," I think. This isn't the time to try to do a tricky touch shot.

I crouch down lower and lower as I track the trajectory of the ball. Our entire season is coming down to this final shot. The next two seconds seem to happen in slow motion. It's apparent that none of the City High players will get to the ball to make the play. We will win the championship if Shelly's shot lands inside the court. But she's put so much spin on the ball, I'm certain it's going to miss the sideline by several inches. But I'm wrong. The ball nicks the inside edge of the sideline, less than half an inch away from landing out-of-bounds. The official raises his hand to indicate a point for West.

Our bench clears as the players run out and pile on top of each other. Stunned, I collapse the final few inches onto the floor. I gasp for air; I must have been holding my breath without realizing it. I begin to sob.

*It's over, we did it!* I've never felt such a release of tension. A hand gently tugs on my shoulder and I turn to see Scott standing there, ready to help me up off the floor. I slowly stand and he embraces and comforts me. We turn to watch the girls celebrating on the court, both of us crying.

We join our girls at the net and begin shaking hands with the City High players. Both teams are crying, but City's tears are for a lost opportunity, our tears are for a lost friend. I reach Erin Muir, and instead of shaking her hand I step under the net and give her a huge hug. I know she's devastated that she couldn't put the ball in play when she was serving for the title. She played a tremendous match, and I hope she can forgive herself.

I shake hands with City's coach, Craig Pitcher, and congratulate him on a great match. He mumbles a quick congratulations, but the crushed look on his face says it all. He knows his team had the match won, but they blew it by failing to make their serves.

Scott and I turn away from the net and head for our bench. My players are milling around in a circle, hugging each other and laughing and crying at the same time. I can't wait to join in, but before I make it to their circle I hear it. "Sweet Caroline....good times never seemed so good." And suddenly there's only one thing that matters to me: I have to find Ernie as I have so many other times this season. I run over to the partition separating the fans from the court. All the parents start pointing and I see him halfway up the bleachers, holding a large framed picture of Line above his head. I climb over the wall and run up the stairs and fall into his outstretched arms as I have so many other times this year. Neither of us can say a word. We're racked by sobs. Finally we pull apart and I look up into his face.

"Get back to your girls, Brez. That's where you belong." He hands me the picture of Caroline. I give him a kiss on the cheek and one final hug and make my way down to the court to rejoin my team.

Squeaks comes over to me. She's crying hard and I place my hands on the sides of her head and we touch our foreheads together. She's been the nurturer all season, but right now she's the one who needs consoling. I tell her I love her and that Caroline would want her to smile and she does, despite her tears. Then I turn around and see Kelley. We look at each other for a moment before I grab her, both of us laughing and crying. "Kelley, I've never been more proud of anyone," I say. "This was only possible because of your strength and determination. I love you."

She just nods, unable to say anything through her tears. I'm sure she feels like a ton of cement has just been lifted from her shoulders.

The announcer begins to introduce the all-tournament team chosen by a panel of coaches: "Alexus Rogers, Kennedy; Maddie Manning, Ankeny; Olivia Fairfield, West; Rachel Rinehart, City; Michaela Nelson, City; and the captain of the all-tournament team and tournament MVP, Shelly Stumpff from West High." Our students burst into song, serenading Shelly with one more verse of "Happy Birthday." She waves to the students as she walks to the middle of the court to receive her medal and trophy, then joins Eunice and the other honorees. I'm so happy for Shelly. She was such a leader for us this season and her maturity on the court was off the charts in terms of her growth since last year's state tournament.

We wait patiently as City High receives their runner-up state trophy. Then it's our turn to be recognized. The six senior starters hold hands as they walk out to accept the trophy, the trophy that symbolizes their journey of grief. The other team members quickly surround them and then Kelley and Anna jubilantly raise the trophy up to the West High fans. I hand Eunice the picture of Caroline and we begin to walk to the other side of the arena to have our championship picture taken. One of the IGHSAU officials in charge of the tournament leans in as I walk past him and says, "Kathy, take as much time as you need."

I nod dumbly. It's amazing that we're not going to be rushed off the court. Normally teams have about twelve minutes to enjoy their victory and then have to give way to the 4A school championship match. We've just been given free rein to share this moment with our fans for as long as we want. I'm not sure that the two 4A schools will appreciate the delay, but I hope they understand the extenuating circumstances involved with our season and this emotional championship.

As the girls make their way past our student section, kids crowd to the front of the bleachers, stick up their hands, and high-five them. The students are crying as much as the team. Eunice has the picture of Caroline raised above her head with one hand and her finger pointing to the sky with her other hand as a salute to her lost teammate. Then we position ourselves for the photographer, the three dozen roses given to us as the winning team set prominently in front and Anna and Kelley holding up Caroline's jersey next to the championship trophy.

When the official photographs are complete, we pick up our trophy and flowers and move off the court to the side of the arena. The girls continue hugging each other and I walk over to meet with the media. Reporters for the state and local newspapers crowd around me, asking questions: "Coach, did you think a state championship was a possibility in August after you lost Caroline?" "What does this championship mean to your girls?" "Will Caroline's uniform number be retired?"

I answer as well as I can. "Back in August, there was no way I could have imagined a state championship was a possibility. At that time, I didn't think playing volleyball was going to be a possibility. These fifteen young women have demonstrated strength and courage beyond their years. What they've accomplished this season is one of the most amazing sports stories of all time. They have awed and inspired me."

As I continue answering questions, I overhear something Erin, City's setter, is saying to a reporter who's interviewing her about four feet away: "It felt like we were playing against seven people on the court instead of six."

Her comment gives me pause, and I realize she's right. Caroline was with us on the court today. Line has been with us every moment of every day. I'm not sure why I haven't realized that earlier. She was present in Shelly's crazy stunts that disrupted practices. She was there when Squeaks gave out reassuring hugs. She was there in Kelley's shy smiles and every time Anna or Eunice or Hannah screamed with excitement after we scored a big point. We felt Caroline's presence every time friends and strangers offered their condolences and support. She hasn't been with us in the flesh, but her spirit has been with us every single day.

My players are breaking into smaller groups. Some are packing up their gear and others roam over to talk to their parents. Off to the side of the arena Hannah's sitting on the floor, pain etched on her face. I walk over and sit down beside her. I put my arm around her shoulder and say, "We did it, Hannah. I'm so proud of you."

She rests her head on my shoulder and says, holding back tears, "This just isn't fair." I know exactly how she's feeling. In a perfect world, Caroline would have been clowning around for the reporters and Ellyn would have been cheering up in the bleachers. My young players have learned one of life's harsh lessons: Life isn't necessarily fair. I put my arm around Hannah's shoulder and we sit in silence. There's nothing I can say to make her feel better.

When we leave the playing court, an IGHSAU official walks over to offer his congratulations. "Kathy, I know we shouldn't have, but every one of us was secretly rooting for your team," he says quietly.

I thank him and am once again reminded of how many people have been there for us this season. Competing teams, St. Andrew's congregation, our West High community. I'm humbled to have been part of such an amazing journey.

I stop and take one last look around the arena before I go out to join my players. Our fans have left the bleachers, but there are still Live Like Line shirts scattered throughout the stands. Complete strangers wore those shirts to support us. I shake my head in awe and walk out of the ice arena.

The girls are mingling with their families, friends and fans in the lobby. Despite the many smiles, photos, and hugs, the celebration is subdued. I know my players aren't allowing themselves to fully enjoy the moment. Their faces reflect their conflicting feelings. They feel guilty about being happy. I worry about what my girls will do without volleyball now that it's over. The goal of winning a state championship for Caroline gave them direction and purpose during the past three months. The volleyball court was the one constant in their lives, the one thing that held them together, and now that lifeline is gone. My hope is that the bonds we've all forged with each other will remain strong and give them the strength they'll need in the coming months and years.

Ninety minutes after the match is over, we board the bus for the trip home. It takes thirty minutes for the bus to get from Cedar Rapids to Iowa City. It's probably the quietest bus ride home a state championship team has ever taken.

# CHAPTER 40

# WELCOME HOME

There are several hundred people waiting in West High School to welcome us home. People aren't here just to celebrate a state championship – they're here to celebrate the entire journey we've all shared. Scott and I follow the girls into the Little Theater. We receive a standing ovation as we walk down the aisle to our seats on the stage. The girls smile, but I can see in their faces that they're almost embarrassed by the attention. Up until this point, most of the attention has focused on Caroline's tragic accident or their ability to play volleyball. Now they don't have the court and their athletic skills to divert attention from them as individuals—all eyes are on them.

Marv Reiland, our athletic director, and Dr. Jerry Arganbright, our principal, each go to the podium and address the crowd. Mainly they talk about the girl's resiliency and determination. I'm reminded of how fortunate I was to have administrators who supported the team and allowed Scott and me as coaches the freedom to manage the girls as we saw best. They knew my first priority this season was attending to the needs of my players. Marv and Jerry also recognized that I was dealing with my own personal grief and allowed me a great deal of latitude as far as attending school meetings and other district requirements.

Ernie's the last person to go up to the podium to speak. He offers to host a victory celebration at the farm and tears well up in my eyes. All I can think about is Ellyn making the same offer after last year's state championship game. Life was so much less complicated and painful then. It seems like a million years ago now. Marv turns on the sound system and the team and I leave the stage to strains of Queen's "We Are the Champions." We share many hugs and congratulatory praises with the people lining up along the aisle to the exit.

Before the girls leave, there's one more thing that I want us to do together. I call them over to where Scott and I are standing. "I think we should have one last official team function before we part ways," I say. "How about we go talk to Line before we head out to the farm?"

Nobody seems surprised by my suggestion. They all nod their heads as if they've been thinking the same thing. I always knew I wanted to do this after our last match of the season. I hope it'll give us all some closure. Our season started and will end at that tree.

We drive our cars down to the University of Iowa soccer fields and park in the same place we parked three months earlier. This time there are no reporters here. It's just us. We join hands and walk the half-mile to the site of the accident. No one says a word. We cross Mormon Trek Boulevard and form a circle around the tree that took our Caroline's life. I'm holding a dozen roses that were presented to us after the match, and Scott has the bag of butterflies.

I hand each girl a rose and we spread the petals around the base of the tree. I put my hand on the rough bark and say a silent prayer: "Number 9, we love you and miss you. I know you were with us every step of the way." The girls all have tears in their eyes and I know they feel the same way I feel.

Scott opens the bag holding our construction-paper butterflies, and one by one the girls dig through the sack to find the particular butterfly they wrote on before the tournament matches. "These butterflies were always going to be for you, Line," I say. "We knew you'd help us conquer our fears." I watch the girls place the butterflies in the branches of the tree and we bow our heads, each of us lost in her thoughts.

As we turn to start back to our cars, I quietly pull Kelley away from everyone. I hand her the beaded metal butterfly. "Kell, you deserve this and I want you to have it. No one could have done what you did."

She looks at me, tears running down her face. "Thanks," she says.

"No, Kelley, thank you." I give her a big hug and we walk hand in hand to rejoin the rest of the team.

## CHAPTER 41
# OUR JOURNEY

Idrive away from the accident site, thinking it feels impossible that our season is officially over. I'm going to miss being around Scott and those fifteen girls. I know that I'm going to have an ache in my heart, a sense of emptiness, every day after school. For the past three months, the best part of my day was walking into that gym and seeing my players.

Charlie greets me at the door and I drop down on one knee and hold him close. Unlike last season, I'm not jumping around and yelling with excitement about winning a state championship. This season is not one to celebrate. I grab a Miller Chill from the refrigerator and step outside. The cool November air is invigorating. I sit down on the glider and Charlie quickly jumps up beside me. As much as I feel sad that our season is ending, I'm surprised that I also feel a sense of relief. It's as if a thousand pounds have been lifted from my shoulders.

Charlie rolls onto his back and I absentmindedly rub his belly, and think about the amazing journey we all—the girls and Scott and I—have taken together.

I don't believe in that old adage that everything happens for a reason. However, I do believe that we can find meaning when tragedy strikes. We can allow our self-pity to pull us down into a vortex of despair, or we can grasp the strands of hope that are always within our reach. No one will ever convince me that Caroline's death was a part of a bigger picture. She was simply the victim of a moped crash. On average, seven teenagers die in the United States every day in a motor vehicle accident. Those seven deaths represent thousands of family members and friends who, like us, are devastated by the loss of a special person.

If someone had told me on August 11, that Caroline's death would end up having a positive effect on thousands of people, I would have said they were crazy. Those August days following her accident were the lowest times of my life. In August, I questioned whether my players would be able to continue the season. They were reeling with grief and yet they were expected to play the very sport that personified their lost friend. Every practice and every match was a constant reminder, especially to the seniors, that Caroline was gone. They struggled and they cried. Yet they pushed forward. Somehow they found an inner reserve that gave them the strength to honor Line with their volleyball playing. How did this group—their innocence shattered—manage to not only survive, but thrive on the court? How did they accomplish all this without their beloved friend and leader? What makes a champion? How do some people, in the face of adversity, rise to unprecedented levels of excellence? I will be forever in awe of those girls. How they masked their emotions in front of their classmates and came to practice each day with a single-minded thought: "We have to do this for Caroline."

No one exemplified this more than Kelley. She didn't want the burden that I put on her shoulders. She didn't want to take Caroline's spot on the court, but she did. She took on the setting role while battling her personal emotional demons in order to help the team. Every day was a struggle, because not only did she have to learn a new position, but she was thrust into a leadership position that she never could have anticipated nor desired.

Somehow my players managed not only to play

volleyball, but to excel. Perhaps more difficult than the physical aspect of competing at an elite level was their emotional burden. They felt they needed to succeed for the West High students and community. The more people that showed up to cheer them on, the more pressure they felt to be successful on the court. Watching these fifteen girls fight through their despair and persevere on the court and in their daily lives has changed me forever.

I'd left coaching in 1999 because I had lost my perspective about the purpose of high school athletics. I was tough on kids and even tougher on myself. This season has taught me that it's okay to be vulnerable, to lose sometimes, and to accept support and help from others. We made it through the loss of Caroline because we all knew that we were experiencing the same feelings and we were there for each other. I also learned the most important coaching lesson of my twenty-six-year career: Players won't care how much you, the coach, know about the game until you prove you care about them as people.

I've come to realize that barriers aren't necessary between players and coaches. I've had great relationships with some of my players in the past, but I've never had the kind of connection I have with my current players. These girls have my utmost respect, admiration and, more importantly, my unconditional love. They know that I'll be there for them whenever they need me, and I trust that they'll do the same for me.

My thoughts are interrupted by a text from Scott. "We're all at the pub. Are you on your way yet?" I smile. I'll have plenty of time in the months ahead to sort out all my feelings.

I turn to my faithful companion. "Come on, Charlie. Do you want to go for a ride?"

## CHAPTER 42

# CELEBRATION AND GRIEF

I carry the state championship trophy into the pub, but unlike the previous year, no cheers greet me upon my arrival. I see that Scott, Ashten, and my best friends have pushed two tables together and that they've already ordered appetizers. Scott smiles and beckons me to the open seat next to him and Ashten. I squeeze through the crowd of regular patrons. A few of them stop me to offer their congratulations on the state title, and many more express amazement at what our girls were able to accomplish this season.

I reach our table and set the trophy in almost exactly the same spot we put it in after last year's championship. A beer is already waiting for me and I raise the bottle to salute my friends and staff. "Thank you, guys, for everything. Without your support, love, wisdom, and encouragement, I know I couldn't have made it through the past three months." We tap our bottles and glasses together and Scott says, "To Line." We all nod and I take a long pull on my beer.

Our group is pretty quiet; this November we're not doing shots and going crazy. Like me, everyone at our table seems to be lost in their own thoughts. I think about all the texts Caroline sent me when we were here a year ago, demanding that we hurry up and get out to the farm and join them. I fight to hold back my tears as I think of her. Sensing my sadness, Scott puts his arm across my shoulders and puts his head against mine. I tightly shut my eyes in a feeble attempt to keep the tears at bay.

Scott pulls his arm away and gets up. I rest my head on my hands and take a deep breath to compose myself. Scott goes off somewhere and comes back with a slight smile. I can tell by looking at him that he's pleased with himself and within moments I understand why. The sweet melodic Neil Diamond song begins to play on the juke box:

*"Where it began, I can't begin to knowing. But then I know it's growing strong...."*

We all stand up and begin to sing, our arms around each other's waist. When the refrain ends and the famous chorus begins, almost everyone in the pub joins us:

*"Hands, holding hands. Reaching out, touching me, touching you. Sweet Caroline, good times never seemed so good."*

I look around the room and see the bar patrons standing with their arms raised above their heads, swaying in unison. I'm sure some of them aren't aware of the significance of that song to our table of ten, but the majority understand, and when the song ends the crowd breaks into applause.

Scott leans over and whispers in my ear. "Line wouldn't want us to be sad today. We owe it to her and our girls to enjoy this moment. It's time to celebrate a remarkable season with our team."

"You're absolutely right, my friend. Thank you." I turn to the rest of our group. "Let's head out to the farm. We have a state championship to celebrate."

We settle our tab and walk out to our cars. I feel much better than I did an hour earlier. I can see Charlie's red snout sticking out the open window and his tail wagging furiously. I unlock the door and push him off the driver's seat. "Come on, big guy, let's go to the farm."

It's already dark at 6:30. A sliver of moon peaks

through the evening clouds and illuminates the cornfields and pastures on each side of Highway 1 as I drive the three miles out of town. When I turn onto the gravel road that leads to the Found farm, I can see the flames of a bonfire reaching five feet into the sky from a half-mile away. The sight of this huge fire makes me smile. I know that Ernie must have used his front-end loader to push a huge pile of timber together for tonight's special occasion. I squeeze into one of the few available parking spots bordering Ernie's driveway. Charlie eagerly jumps out of the car and sprints off to find the Founds' dogs, and I wait for Scott, Ashten, and my other friends who celebrated at the pub, to park their vehicles. I lean against the warm car hood and listen to the bass pumping out of the speakers in the barn.

Now I just want to see my girls having fun. I go to the barn and make my way across the wooden floor, ducking the dangling feet of the rope-swing riders flying past only a few feet above my head. I stop when I see Shirley Fliehler, Kelley's mom, standing at the base of the loft steps.

"Coach," she says. "I can't begin to thank you enough for all you did for all the girls this season. Kelley wouldn't have made it without you. You were just tremendous, and I'm indebted to you forever."

My throat tightens up and I have to wait a moment before answering. "Shirley, what you don't understand is that we got each other through this season. And we did it partly because of you parents, the West High community, and our student body. This was a journey shared by all involved. Thank *you* for all your support this season and if you ever get tired of Kelley, I'd love to adopt her."

We both smile and I give her a huge hug before walking up the steps to the second floor. The kids are dancing and laughing but not with the same exuberance as the previous year. Everything this year is tainted by not having Caroline to celebrate with us. I hang back in the shadows and don't join them on the dance floor, unlike last season. I don't feel as goofy as I did after last year's state championship. I turn to leave and go outside to join the adults when I hear someone call out my name. Allie Hutcheson, Kennedy's all-state player, and several of her teammates come running over. I give her a big hug.

"What the heck are you doing here?" I ask.

With a big smile, Allie replies, "We lost Caroline too and wanted to show our support. We wanted to help you guys celebrate your championship."

"You goof-balls," I say. "Thanks so much for all you've done for us. It means so much to the girls and me that you're here tonight. As far as I'm concerned, you will always be a part of our West High family. I love you."

We hug a second time and she and her friends rejoin the kids on the dance floor. Our team had eliminated Kennedy in the semi-finals and I'm stunned that Allie and her friends came to our celebration. I wipe my eyes and walk out to join Scott and my other friends out by the fire.

Several hours later I'm heading home from the party, Charlie sitting in the front seat beside me and the championship trophy taking up the entire back seat of my small hybrid car. I feel exhausted, almost numb. It's late in the evening, but I can't tell if I'm tired or overwhelmed by emotion.

My car idles quietly as I wait out a red light on the corner of Highway 1 and Mormon Trek Boulevard. Looking around for my phone, I see a construction paper butterfly wing sticking out from under the passenger seat. I had made several extra, and this one must have fallen out of my volleyball briefcase. The light turns green and the car that has been stopped on my left begins to move through the intersection. Without even thinking, I jerk the wheel sharply left and change lanes.

"Short detour, Charlie," I say out loud.

Staying within the 35 mph speed limit, it only takes me five minutes to reach my destination. I pull onto the shoulder of the road next to the University of Iowa soccer fields. The same spot where the girls and I parked six hours earlier.

I snap a leash on Charlie's collar, then reach down for the butterfly, and put it in my back pocket.

"Let's go buddy. We have one more butterfly to deliver." The two of us make our way along the darkened sidewalks to the tree that changed our lives. Its lower branches are covered with construction-paper butterflies—pink ones, purple ones, yellow ones, orange ones—each butterfly carrying the scrawled fears and hopes of one of the fifteen high school girls who mourned and persevered and became survivors and winners. I reach up and pull down the very top branch and wedge the last, navy-blue butterfly between two leaves. I glance at the tree one last time, then I turn around and Charlie and I walk away without looking back.

# JUNE 19, 2015

It's a beautiful Midwestern summer night and the bars in downtown Iowa City are already busy, even though it's only six o'clock. I don't have much experience with bars normally frequented by college students and I've certainly never been on a bar crawl, but I'm about to drink the first drink of a bar crawl tonight. I raise my shot glass.

"Here's to you, Caroline," I say. "I know this would be a wilder night if you were with us to celebrate your 21st birthday."

The fireball burns on the way down and magnifies the lump in my throat. Shelly, Kelley, Squeaks, Scott, and Anna all toss their shots back. No one says anything for almost a minute until Scott breaks the silence.

"Order up another round!"

"Oh my God, not yet!" I say. "We'll all be incoherent in an hour if we do that!"

We're in Brother's, a popular bar with the college students and our first stop of the evening. Our traveling group has five more bars to go. Twenty other parents and kids have joined us here and before the night is over, our number will swell to 100. Most of us are wearing navy blue t-shirts with the words 'Sweet Caroline's Drinking Team' and the number 21, for how old Caroline would be today, printed on the front in Carolina blue. The backs of the shirts are inscribed, in all caps, with the phrase we used so stoically and steadfastly during our unbelievable season: 'Good times never seemed so good.'

I was ambivalent about joining the girls because, to quote Scott, "That's how coaches get fired." But I know this night isn't about drinking to excess, but rather about celebrating the girl who changed our lives forever. Scott, myself, Ernie, the girls, and their parents still celebrate as a group every Christmas season, but it's becoming harder. Now that the girls are getting older, it's becoming more and more difficult to mesh our schedules with their different college schedules and West Point, where Eunice is, doesn't take scheduled breaks like a regular university. Not everyone can make it tonight for the same reason: Hannah is studying in Italy this summer, and Eunice wasn't able to take a leave from the military academy. But Kelley, Shelly, Squeaks, and Anna Pashkova are all here.

Scott and I pull two bar stools up next to each other and sit at the end of the elevated table where we're all congregated. I retired from coaching West High varsity this past season, so I haven't seen him much. We quickly begin to catch up with each others' lives, and Scott regales me with a few anecdotes about his two-year-old son Everett. His blue eyes gleam with happiness as he talks about his new technology job at the University of Iowa hospital—he started a few months ago—and the bigger house he and Sheena are looking to buy.

Our conversation is interrupted by the sound of the girl's laughter. They're mugging for the camera, all the girls trying to fit together into the same selfie. I love seeing them happy and celebrating. I try to sneak into their picture, but Squeaks playfully pushes me away. I start to walk away, pretending that my feelings are hurt, but Squeaks quickly grabs my sleeve and pulls me back into the group for a couple more pictures.

"I miss you," she says.

"I miss you guys too. When I walked in tonight, I

realized that I felt whole when I saw the group, and that that happens every time I see any of you girls."

Squeaks gives me a big hug and I can feel the truth of what I just said. Caroline's death forged a bond between these girls and me that's impossible for anyone else to understand. Between Scott and me too. We all had to be there for each other through the worst of times and the best of times. Now when we're able to get together we spend the first ten minutes hugging and re-hugging and saying how much we've missed each other. As time passes, we've grown even closer and appreciate each other even more.

I watch the girls enjoying themselves now over near the bar. They're laughing, Anna and Shelly are texting, and Squeaks and Kelley have their heads close together sharing some story. They all look more mature. Their faces and bodies have filled out, but anyone could tell they're athletes. Their long, strong legs carry them effortlessly around the room, and their arm definition is still obvious under the sleeves of their blue t-shirts.

But, tonight at least, they're still acting like high school girls. I've noticed that emotionally—when we get together—we revert back to the same roles we had three years ago. Shelly lets loose a huge belch now and begins to laugh as the girls walk back to join Scott and me at the table. Anna, always quiet and reserved, looks at Shelly with disgust and shakes her head. This makes Shelly laugh even louder. Kelley, always preferring to stay out of the limelight, climbs up onto the stool next to me, giggling shyly. Squeaks breaks off from the group, goes over to the door, and greets some more kids who have come to join us with a smile and a warm embrace.

Shelly leans against the table, beside Scott, and I tell her that she's a pathetic weasel just to hear her laugh some more. I tease the girls all the time, about anything and everything—their lack of volleyball skills, their inability to sing, how short the shorts they're wearing are—and they give it right back to me. If I didn't have great self-confidence, I'd feel bad about my height, my clothes, my age, or my hair every time I'm with them.

We banter back and forth, but we've had many serious discussions during these past three years, particularly when I'm with one of them alone. I carefully let them know if I think they're partying too much or making bad decisions, and they don't hesitate to reach out to me when they're feeling down. If they're out of town during those down times their texts or phone calls can come any time of the day or night. Sometimes I simply listen during phone calls as they share how they're feeling—knowing they just need a shoulder to cry on—but there have been times when I've suggested professional counseling and they've followed my advice. Hannah and Squeaks live in Iowa City, and the rest live in various college towns around the country, but come back fairly often to visit family.  It's not uncommon for me to meet up with any one of the girls to eat and talk, whether they're struggling or excited about a new boyfriend or anything in between.

They've been there for me when I needed comforting as well. In January 2014, my father died unexpectedly and I reeled with grief. He had been my support system and my unconditional cheerleader for my whole life. Partway into the visitation at the funeral home in Dickeyville, Wisconsin, I was shocked to look up and see Shelly, Kelley, Squeaks, and Hannah brushing snow off their winter coats as they walked through the door. I stepped out of the receiving line, ran across the room, and grabbed each of them a huge embrace. They'd driven two hours on snowy Midwestern roads to be there for me.

They aren't the young and innocent kids they were three years ago, but I'm proud of the adults they're becoming. They've retained their goofy senses of humor and they're all excelling in college. Kelley's attending Iowa State University, taking classes to prepare for a physician's assistant program, and Hannah's an engineering student at the University of Iowa; both of them will be seniors next year. Despite the rigors of these majors they've both been very involved with Dance Marathon at their respective campuses. This twenty-four-hour dance event raises millions of dollars to help families whose children have cancer and are being treated at the University of Iowa Hospitals and Clinics. Despite the hundreds of volunteer hours it takes to plan and put on this event, both Kelley and Hannah continue to get almost straight A's—just like they did in high school, from which both of them graduated with 4.0 grade point averages.

Squeaks is attending the University of Iowa, and I convinced her to coach one of our sixth-grade Top Dog volleyball teams this year, since our Tuesday night practices didn't conflict with her class schedule. Top Dog volleyball participants are fifth, sixth, seventh, and eighth grade athletes who will someday attend West High. Squeaks is passionate about our volleyball program and is eager to instill West High pride in our future athletes. Her energy is infectious and the kids look up to her. She also had a 4.0 in high school and is on the dean's list now as she studies human physiology before going to graduate school for public health.

Shelly, Anna, and Eunice will be playing their final seasons of college volleyball this fall. Shelly is at Wingate University and Anna is at Gardner-Webb, both in North Carolina, and Eunice is attending West Point. All three have been honored as all-conference selections in their respective college leagues. Eunice injured her ankle last season and couldn't play during the last few months, but she'll be back in the game this coming fall. She was the leading hitter for West Point during her sophomore season. This past fall I took a trip to North Carolina and surprised first Anna and then Shelly by showing up at games they were playing. Anna's game was on Friday and Shelly's was on Saturday, and I drove the forty miles from Boiling Springs to Wingate on Saturday morning. I swore Anna to secrecy so Shelly wouldn't know I was in North Carolina and was going to show up at her game. I was glad Anna's game came first, because I knew there was no way Shelly would have been able to contain her excitement and keep my being there secret from Anna and all her other Facebook friends.

Anna has been the starting libero for Gardner-Webb since her freshman season. She still leaps four feet into the air when her team scores an exciting point. Sitting in the Gardner-Webb bleachers last year, I watched her effortlessly dig up her opponents' hard hits and pass perfect balls. This fall Shelly will also be a four-year starter and her jump serve and lightening quick right arm still score as many points as she did in high school. I watched her perform on the Wingate court with strength and ease, laughing as she high-fived and back-slapped with her teammates after a particularly strong hit for a point, and then pointed to me in the stands.

Tonight, in the bar, everyone's smiling and seemingly having a good time, but it's hard to celebrate what would have been Caroline's 21st birthday. I can tell by the exaggerated laughs coming from the girls that they are as ambivalent about tonight as I am.

Ernie has yet to show and I wonder if he will. I sent him a text earlier in the day that simply said 'Hugs, my friend. You're in my thoughts."

He replied a few minutes later: "Thanks, Brez. I wonder what tonight REALLY would be like...If...Peace in our hearts." His simple message was a reminder that Ernie's grief will always be quadruple what the rest of us feel. In a span of ten days the heart and soul was torn from the Found family.

It's been just as difficult for Gregg and Catharine, Ernie's other two children. Gregg, the most solemn of the Found children, offers up a quick smile when he's with us, but he tends to hang back from the crowd. He still works for ESPN and is now in charge of NBA and WNBA programming. Catharine seems to be searching for her destiny in life after the accident. After graduating from Trinity College in 2012 she lived in Boston, Denver, and Australia. Now she's moved back to Iowa City and living at the farm house with her father. She's taking prerequisite classes with a plan to get a degree as a physician's assistant. Every time I see her I can't help but think about the story she told the congregation at Caroline's visitation.

She said the two of them were driving home and saw a dead deer that had been hit by a car, lying next to the side of the road. They rushed home and gathered up blaze orange clothing—an Iowa deer hunting requirement—and several of their father's shotguns. They drove back to the deer and took turns snapping pictures of each other kneeling next to the dead animal. This was their way, both of them animal lovers, of parodying pictures posted in hunting magazines of men proudly displaying their trophy kills.

Ernie, Catharine, and Gregg get together often, either at the farm or vacationing out East. I'm not surprised that Gregg has come home for Caroline's birthday to support his father and join us at some point during the bar crawl.

When the team got together this past December, I asked Ernie if it was hard to be around Caroline's friends. He watched the girls laughing as they exchanged "white elephant" gifts and sighed deeply. "It's impossible to not see her friends get older and realize that she'll always be seventeen. I can accept, to a degree, what happened to Ellyn, but I'll never accept the other...." His voice faded away.

Ernie has immersed himself with different charity causes. His skills have been "auctioned off" several times and the winning bidders were treated to an evening of his piano playing or magic tricks. When our group gets together at Christmas, I'm always amazed at what an accomplished pianist he is. His large hands fly over the ivories as we all sing our favorite carols. His innate sense of confidence and charisma seem to draw people in. Later tonight when he joins us, people will gravitate toward him, I know, much the way they did toward Caroline.

He's traveled a lot this year, visiting family and friends, and is mulling retiring from his job as orthopedic surgeon. He bought a lakefront cabin in New Hampshire near the base of Mount Monadnock – the mountain that he and Ellyn climbed every year, first as newlyweds and then eventually with their three children. As Ellyn and Caroline's ashes are interned a short distance away in a small cemetery called Cathedral of the Pines, the cabin is an idyllic summer retreat that keeps him close to his girls.

Our group strolls across the pedestrian mall, heading for our next destination, a bar called DC's. I break off from the navy-blue-clad revelers and veer a hundred yards across the brick-paved mall. Today of all days, I need to see the Live Like Line bench sitting at the south entrance of the ped-mall.

The Live Like Line shirts were the beginning of a groundswell of support for the volleyball team, for the school and for the Found family. No matter where you went—volleyball or football games or school hallways—the shirts were everywhere. I initially had a hard time when I saw a student wearing one of those shirts in school, because it was a too poignant reminder of who we had lost. But eventually I swelled with pride that so many other people wanted to honor Liner.

Then something happened at the school, beginning in the fall months of the new school year:  West High began the year of Living Like Line. It wasn't any proclamation or something that was discussed, it simply happened. There was a sense of solidarity that we needed to stick together, as we had all been impacted by Caroline's death. Much of the normal high school drama was conspicuously absent. People treated each other with respect. Students would smile and wave to each other in the halls. Teachers let my athletes leave during the middle of class, no questions asked. And no one worried about the little annoyances of daily life. It was as if we all wanted to keep the essence of Caroline alive by living our lives the way she lived hers.

Jeremiah Anthony, a junior, started sending tweets to the faculty, staff, and students at West, congratulating anyone he saw do something nice like hold open a door for someone or pick up trash dropped in the hallway. The tweets were simple messages like "Thanks for caring about our school," or, "I saw you help that teacher carry those boxes. Way to Live Like Line." No one was exempt. Jeremiah reached out to everyone, janitors as well as principals. If he didn't know someone's name, he'd ask around until he knew who that person was. The texts were genuine and sincerely tried to make the recipient feel good. It wasn't long before Jeremiah realized his messages were helping people and wanted to expand his secret operation. He recruited five other young men to join him and they became known as the West High Bro's. The Bro's' tweets and daily posts on their new Facebook page reached hundreds of people. It made my day when I was tagged with a post that said "Brez you are an awesome teacher. You rock!" The messages were totally anonymous. Despite speculation, it took months before anyone started to guess who the Bro's were. Even Jeremiah's parents were unaware of their son's random acts of kindness until the national media caught wind of the story and the Bro's were featured on Good Morning America.

All of our athletes played with fierce determination and passion that year. The teams seemed compelled to perform better than their talent levels. "Sweet Caroline" became the anthem for every sport, and her #9 was prominently displayed on uniforms, team shirts, and warm-up jackets. Besides volleyball, West girl's basketball and boy's basketball teams, boy's soccer, track, and tennis all brought home state titles. This was an unprecedented accomplishment in the history of Iowa high school athletics.

I sit down on the Live Like Line bench. Three years ago, the Iowa City city council asked local artists to decorate the benches in the downtown area. Ernie's good friend Paul Etre and his son George commissioned a local artist to paint the bench that's located in front of Formosa, a downtown sushi restaurant. In July of 2012, about 75 people—my players, Scott and I, the girls' parents and many supporters—gathered and watched the artist paint the bench bright blue with large orange lettering, just like the Live Like Line shirts. Squeaks painted the seniors' names and nicknames on the bench seat, along with Scott's and mine. The artist said that anybody who wanted to could help paint the bench, and people, including me, went up and added to the bright blue background.

After one year, the harsh Iowa winters caused havoc with the benches, so that colors faded and the paint was peeling off. It was apparent that they would need to be sanded down and repainted each spring. Different artists have been chosen each year since to showcase their creativity with new designs on all the benches except for ours. Paul has asked for, and was granted, permission to have our bench repainted the exact same as before. It's the only original that remains of the thirty that were painted that first season. Caroline's teammates and friends gather there on Saturday nights when they're out celebrating, and they post their newest "bench gatherings" on their Facebook pages.

Now, I sit here on this bench on Caroline's 21st birthday. I think of her every day. When I get to my office at school the first thing I see is the box of letters written by all those sobbing students in our gymnasium on the morning after the accident. Ernie, the girls and I have talked about burning them in a bonfire during one of our gatherings at the farm, but we've never quite gotten around to it. The box has never been opened and no one will ever read the messages that all our kids wrote to Caroline. Those letters were only meant for Line's eyes.

I turn in my seat and gently kiss the top panel of the bench. "Happy birthday, Liner. Thanks for making me a better person." In this moment I almost feel her sitting next to me, one arm draped irreverently over my shoulder. I imagine her laughing and saying, "Thanks, Coach," her blue eyes gleaming happily in the moonlight.

I walk the short distance to DC's. The bar is packed with Caroline's crew. I see Ernie across the room, flanked by Gregg and Catharine, and we wave to each other. The bar is too crowded to make my way over to him, and the cacophony of sound would make it impossible to talk anyway. I'll catch up with my friend on another day. Besides, I'm about ready to head home—this evening has been emotionally draining. I turn to head out the door but I stop when I hear the now familiar voice of Neil Diamond singing "Sweet Caroline." I anxiously search the crowded bar until I see the four people I have to share this moment with. I push my way through the crowd until I get to Kelley, Squeaks, Shelly, and Anna. We stand side by side with our arms around each other, Kelley on my left, Shelly on my right. All conversation stops and everyone in the bar sings "Sweet Caroline" one more time, our voices filling the room and our eyes filling with tears.

# 2011 WEST HIGH VOLLEYBALL ROSTER

#1  Anna Pashkova — senior
#2  Caroline Hartman — senior
#3  Mollie Mason — sophomore
#4  Hannah Fairfield — sophomore
#5  Hannah Infelt — senior
#6  Hannah Harless — junior
#8  Olivia Mekies — senior
#9  Caroline Found — senior
#10 Erin Weathers — junior
#11 Shelly Stumpff — senior
#14 Laynie Whitehead — freshman
#15 Emily Merdinger — junior
#16 Lyn Jehle — junior
#17 Emily Carpenter — junior
#18 Olivia Fairfield — senior
#19 Kelley Fliehler — senior
Cat Rebelskey — manager
Kathy Bresnahan — head coach
Scott Sanders — assistant coach
Ashten Stelken — sophomore coach

# BONUS MOVIE SECTION

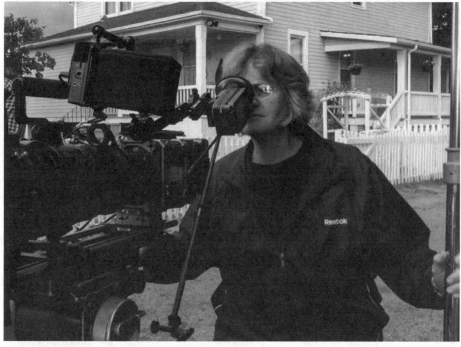

Camera-woman on set in Vancouver - a career change perhaps?

In between leading ladies Erin Moriarty and Helen Hunt.

It was great to finally meet Erin - the sweetest person in the world.

Pete Shilaimon - The heart and soul behind the making of The Miracle Season and the love of my life!

My good friend, Pat Smith, and I asking Erin to autograph her picture in People magazine.

Talking with Helen about an upcoming scene.

Ernie Found and William Hurt enjoying some down time.

# COACH
# KATHY BRESNAHAN
# &
# ACTRESS
# HELEN HUNT
# Q&A

**Helen, you have been in movies that have had physically demanding scenes. Were you an athlete growing up? Did you ever play competitive volleyball?**

*HH: I have done physically demanding roles. I've played a golf pro and a quarterback, I've run from tornadoes. This was not physically demanding. The volleyball players were the ones who played and worked hard. It was emotionally demanding in the best way because the movie is about all the right things. It's about loving people and losing people and how do you go on with joy after you do.*

**Brez, was there a coaching crash course you shared with Helen before shooting began?**

*KB: I was so honored that LD Entertainment would cast such a highly acclaimed actress like Helen Hunt to play the role of Coach Bresnahan and I quickly learned how much is involved in acting. Helen studied my voice inflections, mannerisms, and even how I walked. She would call to ask how I would have felt or reacted emotionally during different scenarios. She morphed herself into a coach and did a tremendous job. I was so touched by her passion and professionalism.*

**Helen, is there added pressure in playing a role where the person you are playing is on set watching you work?**

*HH: Sometimes but there's also a giant well-spring of information to add to what you're doing. When you prepare for a part you're like a blood-hound, sniffing for anything that might help you not make a fool of yourself. Having Brez there to coach my coaching, to speak honestly to me about the sport, her love for these girls and for Caroline was a giant gift an actor rarely gets.*

**Brez, was there ever any discussion of canceling the season after Caroline's tragic death?**

*KB: While I couldn't imagine how we could possibly go on with the season, there wasn't ever a question in our minds to cancel the season. Giving up simply wasn't an option....that would have been a unfair to my players, the community, and Caroline.*

**What are you proudest of about the movie?**

*KB: I'm most proud that LD Entertainment took the risk of producing a movie that featured strong women in the starring roles. This is the first theater movie showcasing female high school athletes and I'm so proud that the world will know my amazing players from that season. They were truly inspirational.*

*HH: I love that I get to be in a movie, standing in a CIRCLE of women reminding them of their power and that it is their birthright to be joyful.*

**What do you hope viewers take away from the movie?**

*KB: I have two dreams: I want people to Live Like Line - treat others with compassion and empathy, live life with passion, and find joy in the smallest things. Also, I want this movie to empower young women everywhere to recognize that they can strong and female - that it should be their goal and something they are proud of.*

*HH: What she said.*